NEW
ENGLAND
FALL FOLIAGE

- - - - - - - - - - - - -

ROAD
TRIPS

D1010389

This edition written and researched by

**Amy C Balfour, Gregor Clark,
Ned Friary, Paula Hardy, Caroline Sieg
and Mara Vorhees**

HOW TO USE THIS BOOK

Reviews

In the Destinations section:

All reviews are ordered in our authors' preference, starting with their most preferred option. Additionally:

Sights are arranged in the geographic order that we suggest you visit them and, within this order, by author preference.

Eating and Sleeping reviews are ordered by price range (budget, midrange, top end) and, within these ranges, by author preference.

Map Legend

Routes

- Trip Route
- Trip Detour
- Linked Trip
- Walk Route
- Tollway
- Freeway
- Primary
- Secondary
- Tertiary
- Lane
- Unsealed Road
- Plaza/Mall
- Steps
- Tunnel
- Pedestrian Overpass
- Walk Track/Path

Boundaries

- International
- State/Province
- Cliff

Population

- Capital (National)
- Capital (State/Province)
- City/Large Town
- Town/Village

Transport

- Airport
- Cable Car/ Funicular
- Parking
- Train/Railway
- Tram
- Underground Train Station

Trips

- Trip Numbers
- Trip Stop
- Walking tour
- Trip Detour

Highway Route Markers

- US National Hwy
- US Interstate Hwy
- State Hwy

Hydrography

- River/Creek
- Intermittent River
- Swamp/Mangrove
- Canal
- Water
- Dry/Salt/ Intermittent Lake
- Glacier

Areas

- Beach
- Cemetery (Christian)
- Cemetery (Other)
- Park
- Forest
- Reservation
- Urban Area
- Sportsground

Symbols In This Book

- ✅ Top Tips
- 🔖 Link Your Trips
- 💬 Tips from Locals
- ↪ Trip Detour
- 📖 History & Culture
- 👨‍👩‍👧 Family

- 🍴 Food & Drink
- 🌳 Outdoors
- 📷 Essential Photo
- 🚶 Walking Tour
- ✖ Eating
- 🛏 Sleeping

- 👁 **Sights**
- 🐚 **Beaches**
- 🏃 **Activities**
- 🎓 **Courses**
- ☞ **Tours**
- ✺ **Festivals & Events**

- 🛏 **Sleeping**
- ✖ **Eating**
- 🍷 **Drinking**
- ☆ **Entertainment**
- 🛍 **Shopping**
- ℹ **Information & Transport**

These symbols and abbreviations give vital information for each listing:

- 📞 Telephone number
- 🕑 Opening hours
- 🅿 Parking
- 🚭 Nonsmoking
- ❄ Air-conditioning
- @ Internet access
- 🛜 Wi-fi access
- 🏊 Swimming pool
- 🥗 Vegetarian selection
- 📖 English-language menu
- 👪 Family-friendly

- 🐾 Pet-friendly
- 🚌 Bus
- ⛴ Ferry
- 🚊 Tram
- 🚆 Train
- apt apartments
- d double rooms
- dm dorm beds
- q quad rooms
- r rooms
- s single rooms
- ste suites
- tr triple rooms
- tw twin rooms

CONTENTS

Fall foliage A Vermont road, ablaze with autumn color

WELCOME TO
NEW ENGLAND FALL FOLIAGE

New England is radiant in autumn, when farm stands overflow with freshly harvested produce and leaves sparkle with brilliant bursts of yellow and red.

These four road trips wend their way through vivid streamers of seasonal foliage. They roam over country roads and circle sparkling lakes, traversing the rolling Berkshire Hills, the forested Green Mountains and the alpine Whites. To see and do the best of New England — to really experience the history, artistry and diversity of this formative region — you have to get in your car and drive.

So rev up your engine. Mount spectacular summits and ogle eye-popping fall foliage. Chow down on crispy clams and fresh farm produce. Turn the page for more.

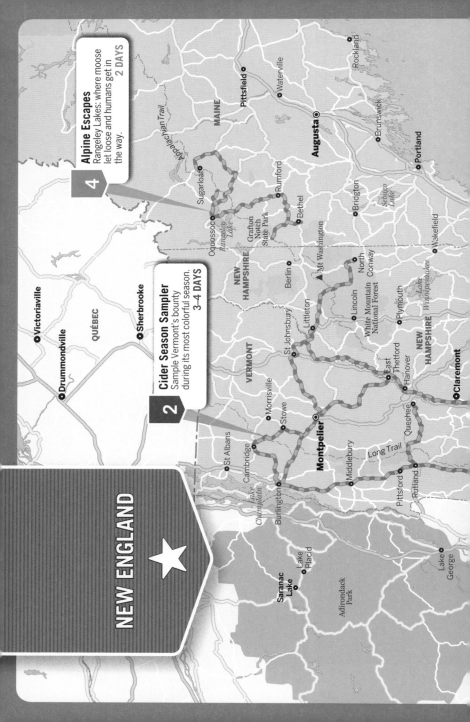

NEW ENGLAND ★

4 **Alpine Escapes**
Rangeley Lakes: where moose let loose and humans get in the way.
2 DAYS

2 **Cider Season Sampler**
Sample Vermont's bounty during its most colorful season.
3–4 DAYS

QUÉBEC

Victoriaville

Drummondville

Sherbrooke

MAINE

Pittsfield

Waterville

Rockland

Brunswick

Augusta

Portland

Sugarloaf

Rumford

Bethel

Oquossoc

Rangeley Lake

Appalachian Trail

Grafton Notch State Park

Bridgton

Sebago Lake

Wakefield

NEW HAMPSHIRE

Berlin

Mt Washington

North Conway

Littleton

St Johnsbury

Lincoln

White Mountain National Forest

Plymouth

Lake Winnipesaukee

VERMONT

Morrisville

Stowe

Montpelier

Middlebury

East Thetford

Hanover

NEW HAMPSHIRE

Claremont

St Albans

Cambridge

Burlington

Lake Champlain

Long Trail

Pittsford

Rutland

Quechee

Saranac Lake

Lake Placid

Adirondack Park

Lake George

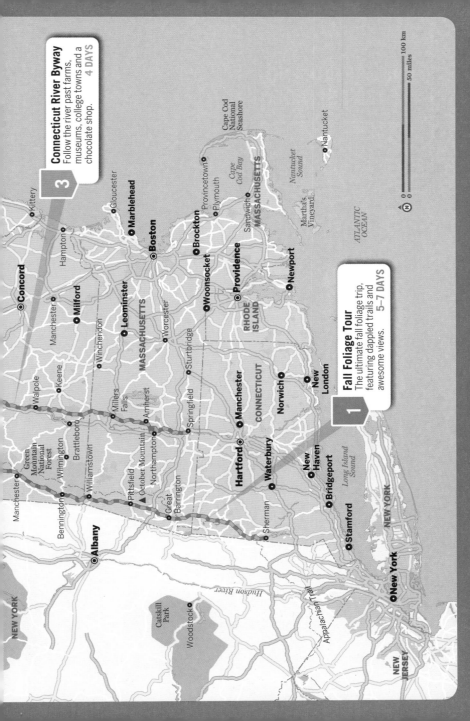

3 **Connecticut River Byway**
Follow the river past farms, museums, college towns and a chocolate shop. **4 DAYS**

1 **Fall Foliage Tour**
The ultimate fall foliage trip, featuring dappled trails and awesome views. **5–7 DAYS**

50 miles

100 km

NEW ENGLAND FALL FOLIAGE

HIGHLIGHTS

★

New England in the Fall (left)
Stop to chug fresh-pressed cider or pluck a patch of berries before the earth goes to sleep under a thick blanket of snow. See it on Trips 1 2 3 4

Appalachian Trail (above)
The AT traverses 14 states and more than 2100 miles. Five of those states and 730 of those miles are in New England. See it on Trips 1 4

Vermont Farms (right)
Vermont farms welcome visitors to learn how they produce the fare that lands on your plate. Experience it to the max when the fall harvest spins into full action and all the leaves erupt in red, yellow and copper. See them on Trip 2

CITY GUIDE

BOSTON

Narrow streets and stately architecture recall a history of revolution and transformation. Today, Boston is still forward thinking and barrier breaking. Follow the Freedom Trail to learn about the past; stroll along the Rose Kennedy Greenway to appreciate the present; and visit the galleries, clubs and student haunts to envision the future.

Getting Around

Park your car and explore the city by foot, bicycle or subway. The USA's oldest subway system, the **MBTA** (www.mbta.com; fare $1.70 to $2), is known on the ground as 'the T.' Boston's fabulous bike-share program, the **Hubway** (www.thehubway.com; registration $5, per hour $2), has 60 stations where you can borrow a bicycle for an hour or a day.

Parking

Street parking is scarce and meter readers are ruthless. Relatively affordable parking lots are located under the Boston Common and in the Seaport District.

Where to Eat

Boston's most famous eating area is the North End, packed with *salumerie* (delis), *pasticcerie* (pastry shops) and ristoranti.

Above Boston Harbor at night

The Seaport District is the place to go for seafood, while Quincy Market is a giant food court that has something for everyone.

Where to Stay

Boston is small enough that almost all of its neighborhoods offer easy access to great sights, dining and entertainment. Beacon Hill and Back Bay are particularly charming. Although the West End is desolate, its hotels offer excellent value given their convenience to Downtown Boston.

Useful Websites

Boston.com (www.boston.com) The online presence of the *Boston Globe*.

Universal Hub (www.universalhub.com) Bostonians talking to each other.

Sons of Sam Horn (www.sonsofsamhorn.net) Dedicated to discussion of all things Red Sox.

Lonely Planet (www.lonelyplanet.com/boston) Destination information, hotel bookings, traveler forum and more.

Destination coverage: p60

For more, check out our city and country guides. www.lonelyplanet.com

NEED ^{TO} KNOW

CELL PHONES
The only foreign phones that work in the USA are GSM multiband models. Network coverage is poor in the White Mountains.

INTERNET ACCESS
Wireless internet access is available at most hotels and cafes, often free. Internet cafes aren't common, but hotels and libraries often provide computers for internet access.

FUEL
Gas stations are ubiquitous and many are open 24 hours a day. Small-town stations may only be open from 7am to 8pm or 9pm.

RENTAL CARS
Dollar (www.dollarcar.com)

Rent-A-Wreck (www.rentawreck.com)

Thrifty (www.thrifty.com)

IMPORTANT NUMBERS
AAA (📞800-222-4357)

Directory Assistance (📞411)

Emergency (📞911)

Climate

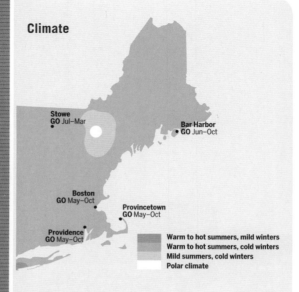

Stowe
GO Jul–Mar

Bar Harbor
GO Jun–Oct

Boston
GO May–Oct

Provincetown
GO May–Oct

Providence
GO May–Oct

Warm to hot summers, mild winters
Warm to hot summers, cold winters
Mild summers, cold winters
Polar climate

When to Go

Mid-October is peak foliage-viewing time, but leaves are turning from mid-September to November.

High Season (May–Aug, Oct)
» Accommodation prices increase by 50% to 100%; book well in advance.

» Expect temperate weather and blooming trees. July and August are hot and humid, except in mountain areas.

Shoulder Season (Apr, Sep)
» Accommodations are less likely to be booked in advance; lower prices may be negotiated (also applies to beach areas in May, early June and October).

» The air is crisp and cool, but blue skies prevail.

Low Season (Nov–Mar)
» Significantly lower prices for accommodations.

» Crowds thin out, but many sights are closed.

» November is chilly and gray, but real winter arrives with snowy skies and icy temperatures from December to March. Driving can be perilous.

Daily Costs

Budget: Less than $100

» Camping or hostel bed: $25–$45

» Meal at roadside diner: $5–$15

» State parks, walking tours: free

Midrange: $100–$250

» Double room in midrange hotel or B&B: $100–$200

» Meal at midrange restaurant: $20–$40

» Museum admission: $10–$20

Top End: More than $250

» Double room in top-end hotel: $200 or more

» Meal at the finest restaurants: $40–$60

Eating

Roadside diners Simple, cheap places with limited menus.

Seafood shacks No-frills seaside venues offering excellent seafood.

Farms Small farm cafes showing off the harvest.

Vegetarians Selections available at most restaurants and cafes.

Eating price indicators represent the cost of a main dish:

$	less than $10
$$	$10–$20
$$$	more than $20

Sleeping

B&Bs Quaint accommodations, often in historic houses, usually including an elaborate breakfast.

Motels Affordable roadside accommodations, usually on the outskirts of town.

Camping Facilities for tents, often at state and national parks. Some campgrounds also offer simple cabins.

Cottages, condos Multi-room units in a resort or complex, usually available for longer stays.

Sleeping price indicators represent the cost of a double room:

$	less than $100
$$	$100–$200
$$$	more than $200

Arriving in New England

Boston Logan International Airport

Rental cars Sumner or Ted Williams Tunnel toll is $3.50.

Silver-Line bus Travels downtown ($1.70 to $2).

Subway Free shuttle goes to blue-line Airport station; subway fares are $1.70 to $2.

Manchester International Airport

Rental cars Take the free shuttle bus to the rental-car offices.

Shared vans Rides (from $39) to southern New Hampshire and northern Massachusetts.

TF Green Airport (Warwick, RI)

Rental cars Take the free shuttle bus to the rental-car offices.

Trains Run to downtown Providence ($5, 20 minutes) and Boston ($8.25, 90 minutes).

Money

ATMs widely available. Credit cards accepted at most hotels and restaurants.

Tipping

Standard is 15% to 20% for waiters and bartenders, 10% to 15% for taxi drivers and $1 to $2 per bag for porters.

Opening Hours

State and national parks are open from dawn to dusk unless otherwise noted.

Bars 5pm to midnight, some places till 2am

Information 9am to 5pm or 6pm Monday to Friday

Restaurants breakfast 6am to 10am, lunch 11:30am to 2:30pm, dinner 5pm–10pm

Shops 9am to 7pm Monday to Saturday, some noon to 5pm Sunday

Useful Websites

Yankee Foliage (www.yankee foliage.com) Excellent leaf-peeping resource, with driving tours and live maps showing the status of the changing trees.

National Parks Service (www.nps.gov/parks) Fast facts about national parks, recreation areas and historic sites.

Visit New England (www. visitnewengland.com) Thorough listing of hotels and attractions.

For more, see the New England Driving Guide (p120).

Road Trips

Driving in the fall, New England
HENRYK T.KAISER/GETTY IMAGES ©

Fall Foliage Tour

1

Touring New England in search of autumn's changing colors has become so popular that it has sprouted its own subculture of 'leaf-peepers.' Immerse yourself in the fall harvest spirit.

TRIP HIGHLIGHTS

212 miles — 7 — St Johnsbury — 8

Lake Champlain
Cruise the lake on a 43ft schooner for the best views

North Conway
FINISH

327 miles

Bretton Woods
Zip-line 1000ft through a golden leaf canopy

● Manchester

75 miles — 5

Mt Greylock State Forest
Magical views from the summit

47 miles

Berkshires
Pack a picnic in the Berkshires' gourmet shops

4

2

Sherman ●
START

10 miles

Kent
Autumn foliage framing the Housatonic River

5–7 DAYS
356 MILES / 573KM

GREAT FOR...

BEST TIME TO GO

August to November for the harvest and autumn leaves.

ESSENTIAL PHOTO

Kent Falls set against a backdrop of autumnal color.

BEST FOR OUTDOORS

Zip-lining through the tree canopy in Bretton Woods.

1 Fall Foliage Tour

The brilliance of fall in New England is legendary. Scarlet and sugar maples, ash, birch, beech, dogwood, tulip tree, oak and sassafras all contribute to the carnival of autumnal color. But this trip is about much more than just flora and fauna: the harvest spirit makes for family outings to pick-your-own farms, leisurely walks along dappled trails, and tables that groan beneath delicious seasonal produce.

❶ Lake Candlewood (p57)

With a surface area of 8.4 sq miles, Candlewood is the largest lake in Connecticut. On the western shore, the **Squantz Pond State Park** (www.ct.gov; 178 Shortwoods Rd, New Fairfield) is popular with leaf-peepers, who come to amble along the pretty shoreline. In Brookfield and Sherman, quiet vineyards with acres of gnarled grapevines line the hillsides.

Visitors can tour the award-winning **DiGrazia Vineyards** (www.digrazia. com; 131 Tower Rd, Brookfield; ⊙11am-5pm daily May-Dec, Sat & Sun Jan-Apr), or opt for something more intimate at **White Silo Farm Winery** (p57), where the focus is on specialty wines made from farm-grown fruit.

For the ultimate bird's-eye view of the foliage, consider a late-afternoon hot-air-balloon ride with **GONE Ballooning** (www.flygoneballooning.com; 88 Sylvan Crest Dr; adult/under 12yr $250/125) in nearby Southbury.

The Drive » From Danbury, at the southern tip of the lake, you have a choice of heading north via US 7, taking in Brookfield and New Milford (or trailing the scenic eastern shoreline along Candlewood Lake Rd S); or heading north along CT 37 and CT 39 via New Fairfield, Squantz Pond and Sherman, before reconnecting with US 7 to Kent.

- - - - - - - - - - - - - - -

TRIP HIGHLIGHT

② Kent (p58)

Kent has previously been voted *the* spot in all of New England (yes, even beating Vermont) for fall foliage viewing. Situated prettily in the Litchfield Hills on the banks of the Housatonic River, it is surrounded by dense woodlands. For a sweeping view of them, hike up Cobble Mountain in **Macedonia Brook State Park** (p58), a wooded oasis 2 miles north of town. The steep climb to the rocky ridge affords panoramic views of

S LINK YOUR TRIP

2 Cider Season Sampler

Hop on Rte 15 out of Burlington towards Cambridge; or head southeast from Montpelier along Rtes 110 and 113 to East Thetford.

3 Connecticut River Byway

Littleton marks the start of this pastoral, river drive.

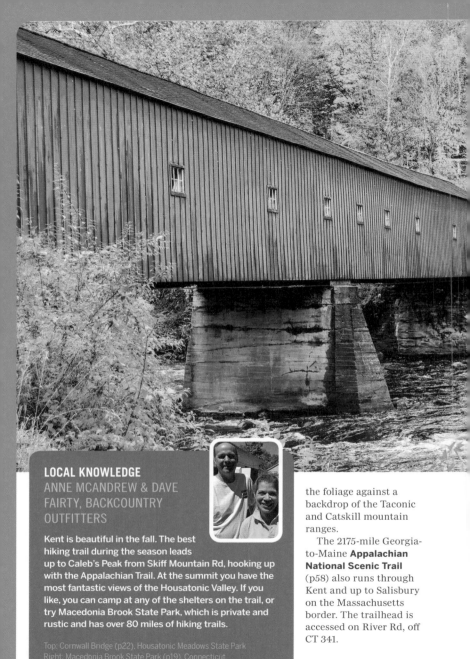

LOCAL KNOWLEDGE
ANNE MCANDREW & DAVE FAIRTY, BACKCOUNTRY OUTFITTERS

Kent is beautiful in the fall. The best hiking trail during the season leads up to Caleb's Peak from Skiff Mountain Rd, hooking up with the Appalachian Trail. At the summit you have the most fantastic views of the Housatonic Valley. If you like, you can camp at any of the shelters on the trail, or try Macedonia Brook State Park, which is private and rustic and has over 80 miles of hiking trails.

Top: Cornwall Bridge (p22), Housatonic Meadows State Park
Right: Macedonia Brook State Park (p19), Connecticut

the foliage against a backdrop of the Taconic and Catskill mountain ranges.

The 2175-mile Georgia-to-Maine **Appalachian National Scenic Trail** (p58) also runs through Kent and up to Salisbury on the Massachusetts border. The trailhead is accessed on River Rd, off CT 341.

TISOPHOTOGRAPHY/GETTY IMAGES ©

DENISTANGNEYJR/GETTY IMAGES ©

The Drive » The 15-mile drive from Kent to Housatonic Meadows State Park along US 7 is one of Connecticut's most scenic drives. The single-lane road dips and weaves between thick forests, past Kent Falls State Park with its tumbling waterfall (visible from the road), and through West Cornwall's picturesque covered bridge across the Housatonic River.

③ Housatonic Meadows State Park

During the spring thaw, the churning waters of the Housatonic challenge kayakers and canoeists. By summer the scenic waterway transforms into a lazy, flat river, perfect for fly-fishing. In the **Housatonic Meadows**

State Park (p59), campers vie for a spot on the banks of the river, while hikers take to the hills on the Appalachian Trail. **Housatonic River Outfitters** (www.dryflies. com; 24 Kent Rd, Cornwall Bridge) runs guided fishing trips with gourmet picnics.

Popular with artists and photographers, one of the most photographed fall scenes is the **Cornwall Bridge** (West Cornwall), an antique covered bridge that stretches across the broad river, framed by vibrantly colored foliage.

On Labor Day weekend, in the nearby town of Goshen, you can visit the **Goshen Fair** (www.goshenfair.org), one of Connecticut's best old-fashioned fairs, with ox-pulling and wood-cutting contests. Also in Goshen is **Nodine's Smokehouse** (www. nodinesmokehouse.com; 39 North St; ⊙9am-5pm Mon-Sat, 10am-4pm Sun), a major supplier to New York gourmet food stores.

The Drive ≫ Continue north along US 7 toward the Massachusetts border and Great Barrington. After a few miles you leave the forested slopes of the park behind and enter expansive rolling countryside dotted with large red-and-white barns. Look out for hand-painted signs advertising farm produce and consider stopping overnight in Falls Village, which has an excellent B&B (p135).

TRIP HIGHLIGHT

④ The Berkshires (p74)

Blanketing the westernmost part of Massachusetts, the rounded mountains of the Berkshires turn crimson and gold as early as mid-September. The effective capital of the Berkshires is **Great Barrington**, a formerly industrial town whose streets are now lined with art galleries and upscale restaurants. It's the perfect place to pack your picnic or rest your legs before or after a hike in nearby **Beartown State Forest** (www.mass. gov/dcr; 69 Blue Hill Rd, Monterey). Crisscrossing some 12,000 acres, hiking trails yield spectacular views of wooded hillsides and pretty Benedict Pond.

Further north, **October Mountain State Forest** (p74) is the state's largest tract of green space (16,127 acres), and is also interwoven with hiking trails. The name – attributed to Herman Melville – gives a good indication of when this

park is at its loveliest, with a multicolored tapestry of hemlock, birch and oak.

The Drive ≫ Drive north on US 7, the spine of the Berkshires, cruising through Great Barrington and Stockbridge. Near Lee, the highway merges with scenic US 20, from where you can access October Mountain. Continue 16 miles north through Lenox and Pittsfield to Lanesborough. Turn right on N Main St and follow the signs to the park entrance.

TRIP HIGHLIGHT

⑤ Mt Greylock State Forest

Massachusetts' highest peak is not so high, at 3491ft, but a climb up the 92ft-high **War Veterans Memorial Tower** rewards you with a panorama stretching up to 100 verdant miles, across the Taconic, Housatonic and Catskill ranges, and over five states. Even if the weather seems drab from the foot, driving up to the summit may well lift you above the gray blanket, and the view with a layer of cloud floating between tree line and sky is simply magical.

Mt Greylock State Reservation (www.mass. gov/dcr; park free, summit $2; ⊙visitors center 9am-5pm, auto road late May-Oct) has some 45 miles of hiking trails, including a portion of the Appalachian Trail. Frequent trail lay-bys on the road up – including some that lead to waterfalls – make it easy

TOP TIP:
NORTHERN BERKSHIRE FALL FOLIAGE PARADE

If your timing is right, you can stop in North Adams for the **Fall Foliage Parade** (www.fallfoliageparade.com), held in late September or early October. Now in its 57th year, the event follows a changing theme, but it always features music, food and fun – and, of course, foliage.

to get at least a little hike in before reaching the top of Mt Greylock.

The Drive » Return to US 7 and continue north through the quintessential college town of Williamstown. Cross the Vermont border and continue north through the historic village of Bennington. Just north of Bennington, turn left on Rte 7A and continue north to Manchester.

- - - - - - - - - - - - - - -

6 Manchester (p107)

Stylish Manchester is known for its magnificent New England architecture. For fall foliage views, head south of the center to 3828ft-high **Mt Equinox** (☎802-362-1114; www.equinoxmountain.com; car & driver $15, each additional passenger $5; ☻9am-dusk May-Oct), the highest mountain accessible by car in the Taconic Range. Wind up the 5.2 miles – with gasp-inducing scenery at every hairpin turn – seemingly to the top of the world, where a 360-degree panorama unfolds, offering views of the Adirondacks, the lush Battenkill Valley and Montreal's Mt Royal.

If early snow makes Mt Equinox inaccessible, visit 412-acre **Hildene** (☎802-362-1788; www.hildene.org; Rte 7A; museum & grounds adult/child $16/5, grounds only $5/3; ☻9:30am-4:30pm), a Georgian revival mansion that was once home to the Lincoln family. It's filled with presidential memorabilia and sits nestled at the edge of the Green Mountains, with access to 8 miles of wooded walking trails.

The Drive » Take US 7 north to Burlington. Three miles past Middlebury in New Haven, stop off at Lincoln Peak Vineyard for

DETOUR: ROBERT FROST COUNTRY

Start: 7 Lake Champlain

Begin this tour at the aptly named town of Middlebury, which stands at the nexus of eight highways. A must-see for microbrewery fans is **Otter Creek Brewing** (p103), north of town.

Drive east along Rte 125, then wind your way up the mountains to the **Robert Frost Interpretive Trail**. At just 1.2 miles, this circular trail is an easy hike marked by half a dozen of Frost's poems mounted on wooden posts along the way, while the surrounding woods and meadows are highly evocative of his work. For information about Robert Frost and more walking trails and several excellent picnic areas, drive less than a mile east of the trail to the **Robert Frost Wayside Area** (on the left).

Continue east on Rte 125 to Hancock then turn right onto Rte 100 south for the blink-and-you'll-miss-it town of **Rochester**, which is worth a stop to experience rural Vermont life minus the masses of tourists in other towns.

Next, head west on Rte 73 to the not-at-all-horrid **Mount Horrid Observation Site** for an essential photo of Brandon Gap from the overlook. When you're done drinking in the views, continue west on Rte 73 to Brandon. Besides the numerous antique shops, restaurants and galleries, the best reason to stop here is the nearby **Neshobe River Winery** (www.neshoberiverwinery.com; 79 Stone Mill Dam Rd, Brandon; ☻11am-5pm Wed-Sun, call for hours Jan-Apr), a friendly wine-and-beer tasting room.

Complete your trip by driving north on Rte 7 back to Middlebury. On the outskirts of Brandon keep your eye out on the right side for Queen Connie, the 19ft-tall concrete gorilla in front of Pioneer Auto Sales.

wine tasting or a picnic lunch on the wraparound porch.

- - - - - - - - - - - - -

TRIP HIGHLIGHT

7 Lake Champlain

With a surface area of 490 sq miles, straddling New York, Vermont and Quebec, Lake Champlain is the largest freshwater

DETOUR: KANCAMAGUS SCENIC BYWAY

Start: ❾ North Conway

From North Conway, the 34.5-mile **Kancamagus Scenic Byway** (p81), otherwise known as NH 112, passes through the White Mountains from Conway to Lincoln in New Hampshire. You'll drive alongside the Saco River and enjoy sweeping views of the Presidential Range from Kancamagus Pass. Inviting trailheads and lay-bys line the road. From Lincoln, a short drive north on I-93 leads to Franconia Notch State Park, where the foliage in September and October is simply spectacular.

lake in the US after the Great Lakes.

On its northeastern side, **Burlington** (p95) is a gorgeous base from which to enjoy the lake. Explore it by foot on our walking tour, p112. Then scoot down to the wooden promenade, take a swing on one of the four-person rocking benches, and consider a bike ride along the 7.5-mile lakeside bike path.

For the best offshore foliage views we love the *Friend Ship* sailboat at **Whistling Man Schooner Company** (p96), a 43ft sloop that accommodates a mere 17 passengers. Next door, **ECHO Lake Aquarium & Science Center** (p112) explores the history and ecosystem of the lake.

The Drive » Take I-89 southeast to Montpelier passing Camels Hump State Park and CC Putnam State Forest. At Montpelier, pick up US2 heading

east to St Johnsbury, where you can hop on I-91 south to I-93 south. Just after Littleton, take US 302 east to Bretton Woods.

TRIP HIGHLIGHT

❽ Bretton Woods (p86)

Unbuckle your seat belt and step away from the car. You're not just peeping at leaves today, you're swooping past them on zip lines that drop 1000ft at 30mph. The four-season **Bretton Woods Canopy Tour** (☎603-278-4947; www.brettonwoods.com; US 302; per person $110; ☉tours 10am & 2pm) includes a hike through the woods, a stroll over sky bridges, and a swoosh down 10 cables to tree platforms.

If this leaves you craving even higher views, cross US 302 and drive 6 miles on Base Rd to the coal-burning,

steam-powered **Mount Washington Cog Railway** (p87) at the western base of Mt Washington, the highest peak in New England. This historic railway has been hauling sightseers to the mountain's 6288ft summit since 1869.

The Drive » Continue driving east on US 302, a route that parallels the Saco River and the Conway Scenic Railroad, traversing Crawford Notch State Park. At the junction of NH 16 and US 302, continue east on US 302 into North Conway.

❾ North Conway

Many of the best restaurants, pubs and inns in North Conway come with expansive views of the nearby mountains, making it an ideal place to wrap up a fall foliage road trip. If you're traveling with kids or you skipped the cog-railway ride up Mt Washington, consider an excursion on the antique steam-powered Valley Train with the **Conway Scenic Railroad** (p79). It's a short but sweet round-trip ride through the Mt Washington Valley from North Conway to Conway, 11 miles south. The Moat Mountains and the Saco River will be your scenic backdrop. First-class seats are usually in a restored Pullman observation car.

Right Fall in the Berkshires (p22), Massachusetts

Cider Season Sampler

2

Vermont is radiant in harvest season, its farm stands overflowing with fresh produce and leaves just showing the first hints of color.

TRIP HIGHLIGHTS

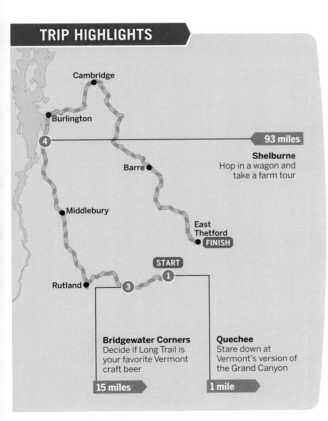

Cambridge

Burlington

4

93 miles

Shelburne
Hop in a wagon and take a farm tour

Barre

Middlebury

East
Thetford
● **FINISH**

START
1

Rutland ●
3

Bridgewater Corners
Decide if Long Trail is your favorite Vermont craft beer

Quechee
Stare down at Vermont's version of the Grand Canyon

15 miles

1 mile

3–4 DAYS
225 MILES / 363KM

GREAT FOR...

BEST TIME TO GO

August to October, when apple-picking is at its prime.

ESSENTIAL PHOTO

Capture the orchards at Shelburne Farms in the early evening light.

BEST FOR FOODIES

Crisp apples from Shelburne Farms and dinner at Simon Pearce (p102) – a divine meal with a view.

Left Quechee Gorge (p28), Vermont

2 Cider Season Sampler

When most people think Vermont food and drink, beer or maple syrup come to mind. But these days, vineyards are brimming with excitement and locavore restaurants are sprouting like mushrooms around the state. Chefs, farmers and communities have begun to work together in mutually supportive ways, and autumn is the best time to embrace the bounty in a blaze of colors.

TRIP HIGHLIGHT

① Quechee (p101)
Vermont's answer to the Grand Canyon, the **Quechee Gorge** is a 163ft-deep scar that cuts about 3000ft along a stream. View it from the bridge or work off those pancake breakfasts with a hike to the bottom – the 15-minute descent through pine forest is beautiful, following a trail on the south side of Hwy 4.

Drop by the **Charlotte Village Winery's tasting**

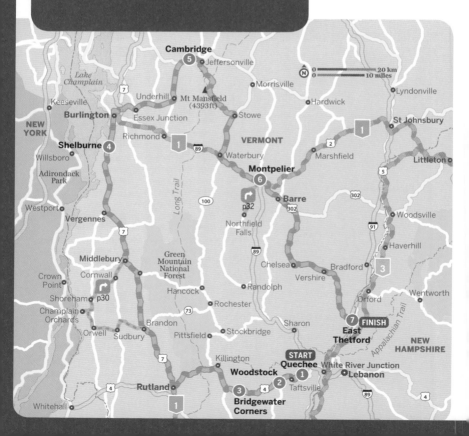

room (3968 Greenbush Rd; ⏱ 11am-5pm), at the gorge parking lot, for free samples of its grape and fruit varietals, such as peach Chardonnay or dry blueberry wine – a remarkably complex, spicy tipple that packs a punch.

In downtown Quechee Village, beeline to **Simon Pearce** (www.simonpearce. com; 1760 Main St; ⏱ 10am-9pm), in the old woolen mill cantilevered out over the Ottauquechee River. Pearce, an Irish glassblower, immigrated to Quechee in 1981, drawn by a vision of running his entire operation self-sufficiently with hydro power. Three decades later, he's built a small empire. His flagship Quechee store displays

LINK YOUR TRIP

1 Fall Foliage Tour

From Burlington, take the I-89 southeast to Montpelier, or pick up the I-93 from Montpelier towards Littleton.

3 Connecticut River Byway

Head east from East Thetford to join the NH 10 towards either Littleton or Montshire.

pottery and glassware and offers glassblowing demonstrations daily.

The Drive » Follow Rte 4 west to Woodstock.

- - - - - - - - - -

2 Woodstock (p101)

Chartered in 1761, Woodstock has been the highly dignified seat of scenic Windsor County since 1766. The townspeople built grand Federal and Greek Revival homes surrounding the oval village green, and four of Woodstock's churches can claim bells cast by Paul Revere. Senator Jacob Collamer, a friend of Abraham Lincoln's, once observed, 'The good people of Woodstock have less incentive than others to yearn for heaven.'

Billings Farm & Museum (p102) employs a mix of 19th- and 20th-century methods. Visitor activities vary with the seasons, from horse and sleigh rides to the afternoon milking of the

cows to demonstrations of making strawberry shortcake in the cast-iron stove.

The **Marsh-Billings-Rockefeller National Historical Park** (p101) contains a mansion with exhibits on environmental conservation and 20 miles of trails. Combined tickets (adult 16-61yr $19) with Billings Farm & Museum are available.

The Drive » Drive west on Rte 4 to Bridgewater Corners, following the curve of the Ottauquechee a few miles upstream.

- - - - - - - - - -

TRIP HIGHLIGHT

3 Bridgewater Corners

Located in an unassuming spot right off the road on the left, **Long Trail Brewery** (www. longtrail.com; cnr Rtes 4 & 100A; ⏱ brewery 10am-6pm, pub food 11am-5pm) is considered by many to be Vermont's number one producer of craft beer. On a sunny day, it's delightful to sit in its riverside beer garden, modeled after Munich's Hofbräuhaus. Inside is a cozy beer hall that's a great place to sample brews. Check out the self-guided brewery tour on the 2nd floor – the small platform explaining the process is worth visiting if you want to know how that frothy goodness is produced. The brewpub serves snacks and meals, but we prefer to stick to the drinks.

The Drive » Continue on Rte 4 west through Killington; you'll cut straight across the Green Mountains. In Rutland, take Rte 7 north to Shelburne.

- - - - - - - - - - - - -

④ Shelburne

In 1886 William Seward Webb and Lila Vanderbilt Webb built a little place for themselves on Lake Champlain. The 1400-acre farm, designed by landscape architect Frederick Law Olmsted (who also designed New York's Central Park), was both a country house for the Webbs and a working farm. These days, the century-old estate and National Historic Landmark exists as **Shelburne Farms** (☎802-985-8686; www. shelburnefarms.org; 1611 Harbor Rd, Shelburne; adult/ child 3-17yr $8/5; ☺9am-5:30pm mid-May–mid-Oct, 10am-5pm mid-Oct–mid-May; 🔆), a working farm and environmental education center.

Tours, in a truck-pulled open wagon, are a barrel of fun: you can admire the buildings (inspired by European romanticism), observe cheese making, and learn about maple syrup and mustard production. Hikers can meander along the walking trails and kids love the animals in the children's farmyard. In mid-September, drop by and celebrate autumn traditions at the annual Harvest Festival, featuring hay rides, a hay-bale maze, music and antique farm machines.

The Drive » Head north on Rte 7 through Burlington (p95). Hop on Rte 15, then Rte 128, then Rte 104.

- - - - - - - - - - - - -

⑤ Cambridge

Even fermented berries have a place in Vermont's food culture. When harvest season is over, some of them go into the dessert wines at **Boyden Valley Winery** (www. boydenvalley.com; cnr Rtes 15 & 104; ☺10am-5pm, closed Mon-Thu Jan-Apr), 20 miles north in the stunningly beautiful Lamoille River valley at the foot of Mt Mansfield. Savor the views and check out the award-winning Gold Leaf, a Vermont-inspired concoction that uses maple syrup straight from the farm combined with local apples.

The Drive » Continue on Rte 104 east to Rte 15 to Rte 100 south. In Waterbury hop on I-89 east.

DETOUR: CHAMPLAIN ORCHARDS

Start: ③ Bridgewater Corners

After passing through Rutland on Rte 7, hop onto Rte 73 west in Brandon and follow the lazy curves of Otter Creek for a couple of miles before breaking into wide open farm country cascading toward Lake Champlain. Just shy of the lakeshore, double back east on Rte 74 to **Champlain Orchards** (www. champlainorchards.com; 2955 Rte 74 W, Shoreham; ☺10am-5pm Jul-Oct; 🔆), where you can pick two-dozen varieties of apples (including many New England heirlooms) or watch the pressing and bottling of ultra-fresh cider. The orchard is famous for its free 'while-you-pick' acoustic concerts and an annual October harvest celebration. After, continue on Rte 74 west until it hits Rte 7 in Middlebury and head north.

Right A farm in Woodstock (p29), Vermont

DANITA DELIMONT/GETTY IMAGES ©

DETOUR: COVERED BRIDGE CENTRAL

Start: ⑥ **Montpelier**

Vermont is rich in these classic beauties, but you generally don't get two (and almost three) for the price of one. From Montpelier, take VT 12 southwest to Northfield Falls to the intersection of Cox Brook Rd, where two covered bridges are within walking distance of each other. **Station Bridge** and **Newell Bridge** both span a section of the river that's about 100ft across. **Upper Bridge** is a bit further up Cox Brook Rd.

- - - - - - - - - - - - - -

⑥ Montpelier (p92)

With 7755 residents, Montpelier is America's smallest capital city and the only one without a McDonald's. It's home to the prestigious New England Culinary Institute (NECI), so stop here for a dose of Vermont history paired with fine food.

Adjacent to the gold-domed **State House** (p92), whose front doors are guarded by a massive statue of American Revolutionary hero Ethan Allen, is the **Vermont Historical Society** (http:// vermonthistory.org; State St; adult/student/senior $12/3/5; ⏰10am-4pm Tue-Sat,

noon-4pm Sun May-Oct). Its award-winning 'Freedom and Unity' exhibit walks you through 400 years of Vermont history. From your first few steps into an Abenaki wigwam, you're asked to consider the true meaning of this state motto. Controversies aren't brushed under the rug, either: a short film presents the early-20th-century debate over women's suffrage alongside footage from the 1999 statehouse hearings where citizens voiced their support or opposition to civil unions. In a very Vermontish way, you're invited to ponder issues on your own (rather than

assenting to someone else's party line). The panoply of voices and imaginative presentation keep this exhibit fun and lively.

The Drive ⟫ Next, head southeast along Rtes 110 and 113 to the Connecticut River in East Thetford.

- - - - - - - - - - - - - -

⑦ East Thetford

Like a roadside farm stand on organic steroids, **Cedar Circle Farm** (www.cedarcirclefarm. org; Pavilion Rd; ⏰10am-6pm Mon-Sat, to 5pm Sun; 🚻) offers endless opportunities to appreciate Vermont's summer bounty: pick-your-own strawberries, blueberries, flowers and pumpkins, and the opportunity to wander through lush fields of produce or lounge in an Adirondack chair by the river. Summer and fall events include dinners in the field, workshops on canning and freezing, and strawberry (June) and pumpkin (October) festivals.

The Drive ⟫ Hop on I-91 south, then I-89 north to return to Quechee.

Right State House, Montpelier

DANITA DELIMONT/GETTY IMAGES ©

Connecticut River Byway

3

This drive links mill towns, white-clapboard villages and colleges as it unfurls beside farms, forests and the Connecticut River, which roars then ripples through New Hampshire and Massachusetts.

TRIP HIGHLIGHTS

1 mile

Littleton
The world's longest candy counter sells gummy eggs!

1 START

● Orford

2 ────── **98 miles**

Montshire Museum of Science
Touch the tooth of a mastodon

● Claremont

172 miles ────── **5**

Walpole
Dawdle over a double-shot mocha at Burdick Chocolate

● Hinsdale

7 ────── **230 miles**

Amherst
Visit the Emily Dickinson Museum, where hope is the thing with feathers

271 miles ── **10 FINISH**

Springfield
The Cat in the Hat steps out of his book at the Dr Seuss garden

**4 DAYS
271 MILES / 436KM**

GREAT FOR...

BEST TIME TO GO
April to November for spring flowers, summer greenery and fall foliage.

📷 **ESSENTIAL PHOTO**

We looked! And we saw him! The Cat in the Hat!

✓ **BEST FOOD**
Dig into fancy chocolates and savory fare at Burdick Chocolate in Walpole.

Left Smith College (p42), Massachusetts

35

3 Connecticut River Byway

Taking a road trip beside the Connecticut River is like earning a liberal arts degree in one weekend. There's Fort at No 4's Colonial history; natural sciences and wildlife at the Montshire; poetry from Emily Dickinson in Amherst; and a mini session in the arts among the sculpture-dotted grounds of Saint-Gaudens. And you'll surely feel like one of the students while strolling the lively campuses of Amherst, Smith and Mt Holyoke.

TRIP HIGHLIGHT

❶ Littleton, New Hampshire (p84)

Littleton may be off the beaten path, but it's an inspirational place to start this trip. The White Mountains hover to the southeast. The Ammonoosuc River churns through town. A towering steeple overlooks Main St. And the world's longest candy counter beckons with a rainbow's array of sweets at **Chutters** (www.chutters. com; 43 Main St; ☺9am-6pm Mon-Sat, 10am-6pm Sun).

At the eastern end of Main St, the **Littleton Chamber of Commerce Visitor Center** (☎603-444-6561; www. littletonareachamber.com; 2 Union St; ☺9am-5pm Mon-Fri) provides a walking-tour brochure. The tour stops at the **Littleton Grist Mill**. Built in 1797, it's back in service as a mill after renovations initiated in the 1990s. The adjacent Ammonoosuc drops 144ft as it crashes through town. The **covered bridge** here, built in 2004, looks like it's barely hanging on to the riverbank – but it's perfectly safe for walking.

The Drive » Take I-93 north to exit 44 and NH 135 south. This bucolic road passes fields, red barns and cattle-crossing signs as it hugs the river. Snap a photo of the covered bridge in

LITTLETON: SHOPPING ON MAIN STREET

Littleton's Main St is lined with indie-owned stores. For outdoor gear and clothing, step into **Lahout's** (www. lahouts.com; 99 Main St; ☺9:30am-5:30pm), America's oldest ski shop. A few doors down is **Village Book Shop** (www.booksmusictoys.com; 81 Main St; ☺9am-5pm), with lots of local and regional books. Downstairs, the **League of New Hampshire Craftsmen** (☺10am-5pm) runs a gallery that sells jewelry, pottery, and other arts and crafts made in New Hampshire.

Woodsville, then continue south on NH 10. In Orford, look left for the Seven Ridge Houses. Built by local craftspeople between 1773 and 1839 in the Bulfinch style, they're impressive. Continue south on NH 10 into Hanover, following it past the Dartmouth green. Take NH 10A/W Wheelock St over the Connecticut River, then take the first left onto Montshire Rd.

TRIP HIGHLIGHT

2 Montshire Museum of Science, Norwich, Vermont

Rub the tooth of a mastodon. View current images from the Hubble telescope. Watch leafcutter ants at work. But whatever you do at the **Montshire** (☎802-649-2200; www.montshire. org; 1 Montshire Rd; adult/child $12/10; ⏰10am-5pm; 🚻), don't park your car near

LINK YOUR TRIP

1 Fall Foliage Tour

Trip 1 runs through Littleton; head west to follow the tour backwards or east for Bretton Woods.

2 Cider Season Sampler

Trip 2 starts and finishes just off the NH10. To join it, turn right onto E Thetford Rd, about 7 miles after Orford, or cross into Vermont at White River Junction.

LOCAL KNOWLEDGE
BOB RAISELIS, EXHIBITS DIRECTOR, MONTSHIRE MUSEUM OF SCIENCE

We have about 3 miles of trails at the Montshire, and all along these trails are exhibits about plants, the ecology of the area, the geology of the Upper Valley, natural history and human history. One really lovely trail is the River Loop. The riverside section is accessible, so it's great for visitors in wheelchairs and those using walkers or strollers. Just past our meadow the riverside section begins, and visitors can walk along the Connecticut River for quite a while, on a gentle sun-dappled trail.

the planet Neptune – it's part of the model solar system that stretches the length of the parking lot and beyond, and Neptune is way, way out there. Located on a 110-acre site beside the Connecticut River, the museum offers exhibits covering ecology, technology, and the natural and physical sciences. It's also the regional visitor center

Top: *Dr Seuss and the Cat in the Hat* designed by Lark Grey Dimond-Cates, and created by Ron Henson, Dr Seuss National Memorial Sculpture Garden (p42)
Right: Native American statue at Native Views shop on the Mohawk Trail (p41)

for the **Silvio Conte National Fish & Wildlife Refuge** (www.fws.gov/refuge/silvio_o_conte) – look for the life-size moose and the displays that highlight local flora and fauna. In summer water-focused and sensory exhibits in the Montshire's outdoor Science Park will fascinate younger kids. The museum is kid friendly, but adults can learn a lot too, particularly from the upper floor exhibits.

The Drive » Return to Hanover, taking NH 10 past the strip-mall wasteland of West Lebanon, where you pick up NH 12A south to Saint-Gaudens. For variety, the river can be tracked along US 5 in Vermont between a village or two, with regular bridges connecting New Hampshire and Vermont until you reach Walpole.

③ Saint-Gaudens National Historic Site, New Hampshire

In the summer of 1885, the sculptor Augustus Saint-Gaudens rented an old inn near the town of Cornish and came to this beautiful spot to work. He returned summer after summer and eventually bought the place in 1892.

39

The **estate** (www.nps.gov/saga; 139 St Gaudens Rd, Cornish; adult/child $5/free; ⏰9am-4:30pm May-Oct), where he lived until his death in 1907, is now open to the public. Saint-Gaudens is best known for his public monuments, including the Robert Gold Shaw Memorial across from the state house in Boston. Recasts of his greatest sculptures dot the beautiful grounds. Visitors can also tour his home and wander the studios where artists-in-residence sculpt. Exhibit buildings are closed in winter, but the visitor center is usually open from 9am to 4:15pm weekdays.

The Drive ›› About 1.5 miles south is the 1866 Cornish Windsor Bridge, the longest wooden bridge in the US. And, yes, you can drive across it. Not quite a mile south, bear left onto Town House Rd at the fork for two more covered bridges, then continue south on NH 12A, which soon rejoins NH 12.

- - - - - - - - - - - - - -

➍ Fort at No 4, Charlestown, New Hampshire

Named for a 1700s land grant, the original fort was built in the 1740s to protect pioneer farmers from the French and Native Americans. The original fort, which was no longer needed by the late 1770s and no longer exists, was reconstructed in the 1960s as a **living history museum** (☎603-826-5700; www.fortat4.com; 267 Springfield Rd; adult/child 6-12yr/youth 13-17yr $10/5/7; ⏰10am-4:30pm Mon-Sat, to 4pm Sun May-Oct). Its layout is based on a detailed drawing sketched in 1746. Visitors can explore the different rooms of the fort, wander the riverside grounds and watch re-enactors, whose activities vary weekend to weekend. Check the Fort at No 4 Facebook page for current activities.

The Drive ›› Views of rolling mountains and hills, as well as fields, railroad tracks, river views and a sugarhouse, decorate the 14-mile drive on NH 12 south to Walpole.

- - - - - - - - - - - - - -

TRIP HIGHLIGHT

➎ Walpole, New Hampshire

Locals descend from surrounding villages to dine at **Burdick Chocolate** (www.burdickchocolate.com; 47 Main St; lunch $13-23, dinner $16-24, desserts $5; ⏰7am-6pm Mon, 7am-9pm Tue-Sat, 7:30am-6pm Sun). Originally a New York City chocolatier, Burdick opened this sophisticated chocolate shop and cafe to showcase its desserts. These carefully crafted treats look like they attended finishing school – no slovenly lava cakes or naughty whoopie pies here. But you'll find more than just rich chocolate indulgences. The adjoining bistro serves creative New American dishes, plus artisanal cheeses and top-notch wines. The creamy quiche is fantastic.

Purchase local art and crafts across the street at the **Walpole Artists Cooperative** (www.walpoleartisans.org; 52 Main St; ⏰10am-5pm Wed-Sat, 11am-3pm Sun), then cross Westminster St for a gander at **Ruggles & Hunt** (www.rugglesandhunt.com; 8 Westminster St; ⏰10am-6pm Mon-Sat, noon-5pm Sun), an eclectic boutique with toys, women's clothes and home furnishings.

The Drive ›› Return to NH 12. Drive south 5 miles to the junction of NH 12 and NH 63 at the sugarhouse. Bear right onto NH 63 for a particularly scenic spin past the Park Hill Meetinghouse and Spofford Lake. Continue across NH 9. After Hinsdale, NH 63 swings back toward the river and soon crosses into Massachusetts. Follow MA 63 south 15 miles. Turn right at Center St and follow it to Greenfield Rd.

- - - - - - - - - - - - - -

➏ Montague, Massachusetts

Montague is beloved for 'books you don't need in a place you can't find.' Luckily, both claims are slightly exaggerated.

On an unassuming road in a sleepy town, the **Montague Bookmill** (www.montaguebookmill.com; 440 Greenfield Rd; ⏰10am-6pm) is a converted cedar gristmill from 1842 that now contains a big used bookstore. The maze of rooms has oodles of used books (many academic and esoteric) and couches on which to read them.

The westward-facing windows overlook the roiling Sawmill River and its glorious waterfall. There are outside decks over the water where you can take your coffee.

Though the bookstore is the biggest draw, there is also an art gallery, a music shop, a cafe and a restaurant that make it even easier to while away half a day at the mill.

The Drive » Leaving the mill, take a left on Greenfield Rd and an immediate left on Meadow Rd, which winds along the river, passing through scenic farmland. At the terminus, turn right on MA 47 to continue south. In Sunderland, turn left on MA 116 and continue about 10 miles into Amherst. For a quicker trip from the mill, head south on MA 47 and continue for 8 miles on MA 63 into Amherst.

- - - - - - - - - -

TRIP HIGHLIGHT

➐ Amherst, Massachusetts (p73)

Amherst is a sleepy little town that exudes academia. That is thanks mostly to the prestigious **Amherst College** (www. amherst.edu), a pretty 'junior Ivy' that borders the town green. Founded in 1821 Amherst College has retained its character and quality partly by maintaining its small size (1600 students).

Nearby, some pretty wooded grounds contain the two stately homes that constitute the **Emily Dickinson Museum** (www. emilydickinsonmuseum.org; 280 Main St; adult/child $8/4;

DETOUR: MOHAWK TRAIL

Start: ➏ Montague, Massachusetts

For the finest fall foliage drive in Massachusetts, head west on MA 2 from Greenfield to Williamstown on the 63-mile route known as the **Mohawk Trail** (www. mohawktrail.com). The lively Deerfield River slides alongside, with roaring, bucking stretches of white water, which turn leaf-peeping into an adrenaline sport for kayakers.

Start your tour in **Historic Deerfield Village** (www.historic-deerfield.org; Old Main St; adult/child $12/5; ⏱9:30am-4:30pm Apr-Nov), an enchanting farming settlement that has escaped the ravages of time. Old Main St now presents a noble prospect: a dozen houses dating from the 1700s and 1800s, well preserved and open to the public. Stop in tiny but charming **Shelburne Falls** (p72) for its art galleries and coffee shops, then seek an adrenaline rush in Charlemont at **Zoar Outdoor** (p73), which offers canoeing, kayaking and whitewater rafting.

Next, head to the Western Summit (2100ft), also known as Perry's Peak, for amazing views of the surrounding Hoosac Range. Allow at least four hours for the hike; if you're short on time the 1.5-mile loop to Sunset Rock is a shorter alternative.

Back in the car, the Mohawk Trail descends quickly, with an exhilarating spin around the Hairpin Turn to make your heart beat a little faster on the way to North Adams. The highlight of beautiful and bleak North Adams is **MASS MoCA** (www.massmoca.org; 87 Marshall St; adult/child $15/5; ⏱10am-6pm Jul & Aug, 11am-5pm Wed-Mon Sep-Jun), a contemporary-art museum of staggering proportions, housed in the former Sprague Electric Company buildings.

Continuing on to Williamstown will link your trip with the Fall Foliage Tour (see p17).

⏱10am-5pm Wed-Sun). Here, the poet lived out her years in near seclusion, penning thousands of poems.

A few miles south of the town center, **Hampshire College** (www.hampshire.edu) is an innovative center of learning, emphasizing multidisciplinary, student-led study. Stop by on your way out of town to visit the **Eric Carle Museum of Picture Book Art** (www.picturebookart.org; 125 W Bay Rd; adult/child $9/6;

10am-4pm), **located on campus.** Cofounded by the author and illustrator of *The Very Hungry Caterpillar,* this superb museum celebrates the art of book illustration with exhibits and a hands-on art studio.

The Drive >> Head west on MA 9, departing Amherst and passing through the strip-mall town of Hadley. Cross the art-deco Calvin Coolidge Bridge (named for a former resident of Northampton), which yields lovely views of the Connecticut River and the Berkshire foothills. Continue east on MA 9 past the Three County Fairgrounds and into Northampton, where MA 9 becomes Main St.

8 Northampton, Massachusetts (p70)

In a region famous for its charming college towns, you'd be hard-pressed to find anything more appealing than the crooked streets of downtown Northampton. Old redbrick buildings, idealistic street musicians and lots of pedestrian traffic provide a lively backdrop as you wander into record shops, coffeehouses, rock clubs and bookstores.

Move a few steps west of the picturesque commercial center and you'll stumble onto the bucolic grounds of **Smith College** (p71). Stroll around the pond, then stop by the **Lyman Conservatory** (www.smith. edu/garden; 15 College Lane;

donation $1; 8:30am-4pm). Visitors are welcome to explore the college's collection of Victorian greenhouses and botanical gardens, which are packed to the brim with beautiful things in bloom.

The Drive >> Drive east on MA 9 and cross the Calvin Coolidge Bridge. On the east bank, veer right onto Bay Rd for about 2 miles, then turn right to head south on MA 47. The road follows the winding Connecticut River for about 6 miles, passing Skinner State Park and Bachelor Brook Resource Area before entering South Hadley.

9 South Hadley, Massachusetts

The southernmost and sleepiest of the area's college towns, South Hadley's tiny center contains a gazebo-dotted green with attendant brick church. Across the street, the urbanist open-air shopping mall is known as the Village Commons. Otherwise, there's not much to see in town, save the beautiful, bucolic campus of **Mt Holyoke College** (www.mtholyoke.edu), the nation's oldest women's college. Laid out by the great American landscape architect Frederick Law Olmsted, the 800-acre campus contains lush botanic gardens, woodland trails and several waterfalls, making it a delightful strolling destination.

Don't miss the gothic **Abbey Chapel,** which contains an impressive handcrafted organ.

The Drive >> Head south out of town on College St (MA 116). Continue south on US 202 to I-91, which will take you south to Springfield.

TRIP HIGHLIGHT

10 Springfield, Massachusetts (p70)

Start at the **Museum Quadrangle** (www.springfield museums.org; 21 Edwards St; adult/child/senior & student $12.50/6.50/9; 10am-5pm), an attractive complex which includes two art museums, a history museum and a science museum. You'll find such diverse attractions as an extensive collection of samurai armor, a mint collection of locally produced Indian motorcycles and an impressive Dinosaur Hall. The highlight is the **Dr Seuss National Memorial Sculpture Garden** (p70), at the center of the complex, dedicated to Springfield's favorite native son.

Besides the children's literary master, another American cultural icon has its birthplace here: basketball. Sports fans should swing by the **Naismith Memorial Basketball Hall of Fame** (p70), located south of the center on the riverfront.

Right Mt Holyoke College, Massachusetts

Alpine Escapes

4

This trek feels akin to flying. Leafy byways soar up the sides of mountains. Pristine forests float beneath lofty overlooks. And bumpy frost heaves add swoop-de-doo turbulence on the back roads.

TRIP HIGHLIGHTS

68 miles

Height of Land
Enjoy sweeping views of Mooselookmeguntic Lake

93 miles

Rangeley Lakes Trails Center
Nordic skiing and hiking on wooded lakeside trails

Oquossoc

6

Sugarloaf

4

Small Falls

Houghton

2

Mexico

3

18 miles

Grafton Notch State Park
Inspire your inner artist at beautiful Screw Auger Falls

1

Bethel
A stylish base camp for multi-season adventure

1 mile

Rumford
We hear that Paul Bunyan has a crush on the *Statue of Liberty*

43 miles

2 DAYS
160 MILES / 257KM

GREAT FOR...

BEST TIME TO GO
June through March is good for hiking, leaf-peeping and skiing.

ESSENTIAL PHOTO
Frame a shot of Mooselookmeguntic Lake from the Height of Land overlook.

BEST FOR WILDLIFE
ME 16 between Rangeley and Phillips is a local moose alley.

Left Screw Auger Falls (p47), Grafton Notch State Park

4 Alpine Escapes

The first time you see a moose standing on the side of the road, it doesn't seem unusual. You've been prepped by all of the moose-crossing signs. But then it registers. 'Hey, that's a moose!' And you simultaneously swerve, slam on the brakes and speed up. Control these impulses. Simply stop and enjoy the gift of wildlife until it moves on. Then share your good fortune on social media, of course.

TRIP HIGHLIGHT

1 Bethel (p118)
If you glance at the map, tiny Bethel doesn't look much different from the other towns scattered across this alpine region. But look more closely. The town is cocooned between two powerful rivers, and several ski resorts and ski centers call the community home. Four state and national scenic byways begin within an 85-mile drive (see p47).

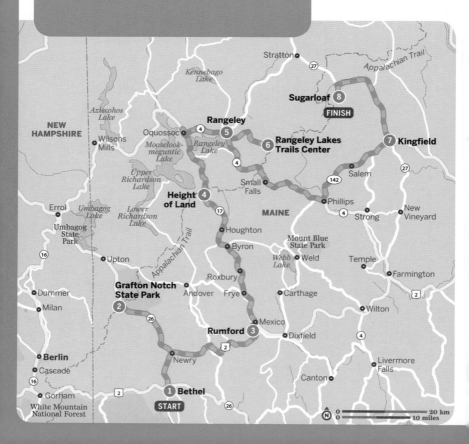

Six miles north of Bethel along ME 5/26, **Sunday River Ski Resort** (📞207-824-3000; www. sundayriver.com; 15 South Ridge Rd, Newry; ski lift adult/ child $80/68; 🚡) lures skiers during winter, with eight peaks, 132 trails, 15 lifts, and a host of activities. In the autumn the resort offers a variety of non-ski activities, such as chair-lift rides, disc golf, ATV tours and canoeing, all of which are excellent ways to view the Fall foliage. From July until early October, the resort opens 30 mountain-bike trails and runs trips up to North Peak on its fast-moving **Chondola** (adult/child $12/8; ⏱10am-4pm Fri-Sun). There's also a six-line **zip-line tour** (tickets $49; ⏱9am, noon & 3pm Thu-Sun).

The Drive ≫ Follow ME 5/ ME 26/US 2 north from Bethel, tracking the Sunday River about 6 miles north. Keep left on ME 26 as it leaves ME 5/ US 2 and becomes Bear River Rd, which leads to the park 11 miles west.

- - - - - - - - - - -

TRIP HIGHLIGHT

② Grafton Notch State Park

Tucked beside the Grafton Notch Scenic Byway within the Mahoosuc Range, this rugged **park** (⏱May 15-Oct 15 207-824-2912, low season 207-624-6080; www. maine.gov; Bear River Rd) is

SCENIC BYWAYS IN THE LAKES & MOUNTAINS REGION

Grafton Notch Scenic Byway From Bethel, follow ME 5/26 north, then take ME 26 toward Grafton Notch State Park at Newry.

Pequawket Trail Scenic Byway Follow the Androscoggin River west from Bethel on US 2. Turn south onto ME 113 at Gilead and follow it to Fryeburg.

State Route 27 Scenic Byway From stop 7, in Kingfield, follow ME 16/27 to Sugarloaf, then continue north on ME 27 to Canada.

Rangeley Lakes National Scenic Byway Drive east on US 2 from Rumford to Mexico, then turn north on US 17. The byway begins about 15 miles north, just beyond the town of Byron.

a stunner. Carved by a glacier that retreated 12,000 years ago, the notch is a four-season playground, chock-full of waterfalls, gorges, lofty viewpoints and hiking trails, including 12 strenuous miles of the **Appalachian Trail**. Peregrine falcons build nests in the cliffs, helping the park earn its spot on the **Maine Birding Trail** (www. mainebirdingtrail.com); the best viewing is May to October. Cross-country skiers and snowshoers enjoy the park in winter. If you're short on time, simply wander the trail beside **Screw Auger Falls**, off the main parking lot. This 23ft waterfall crashes dramatically through a narrow gorge. If you have more time, try the 2.2-mile round-trip hike up

to **Table Rock overlook** or the walk to **Eyebrow Loop** and **Cascade Falls**; there are excellent picnicking opportunities beside the falls.

The Drive ≫ Return to US 2 north. On the 16-mile drive, you'll pass stone walls and antique stores, and enjoy the Androscoggin River tagging along on your right.

- - - - - - - - - - -

TRIP HIGHLIGHT

③ Rumford

How do you know you've arrived? When the giant, ax-wielding **Paul Bunyan** says 'Hey there.' According to legend, the red-shirted lumberman was born in Maine but was later sent west by his parents. Today, he stands tall beside the **River Valley Chamber of Commerce Visitor Center** (📞207-364-3241; www.rivervalleychamber.

com; 10 Bridge St; ⏰9am-5pm daily May-Oct, 10am-2pm Mon-Sat Nov-Apr). Walk a few steps beyond the visitor center building for a fantastic view of the wild and woolly **Pennacook Falls**. The highest falls east of Niagara, they drop 176ft over a granite ledge. The small park here holds a black marble memorial honoring local son and former US senator Edmund Muskie, who authored the Clean Water Act.

The Drive » Leave Rumford and US 2, picking up ME 17 north in Mexico. From here ME 17 runs parallel to pines, farms, meadows and the rocky Swift River. Snap a photo of the river barreling through metamorphic rock at the Coos Canyon Rest Area in Byron, then swoop-de-doo north (you'll see), picking up the Rangeley Lakes National Scenic Byway north of Houghton.

TRIP HIGHLIGHT

❹ Height of Land

The entrance to this photogenic **overlook** sneaks up on you – it's on the left as you round a bend on Brimstone Mountain, just after a hiker warning sign. But don't slam on your brakes and swerve across the grass divider if you miss the turn (we saw this happen), because there's another entrance just north. But you should pull

over. The expansive view of island-dotted **Mooselookmeguntic Lake**, the largest of the Rangeley Lakes, as it sweeps north towards distant mountains is astounding. Views of undeveloped forest stretch for up to 100 miles; you can even see the White Mountains in New Hampshire. The dogged **Appalachian Trail** runs alongside the viewpoint, and an interpretive sign shares a few details abut the 2179-mile footpath.

The Drive » Drive north to the village of Oquosocc, then turn right onto ME 4/16. Take a photo at the Rangeley Lake overlook, where there is a panoramic view of Rangeley Lake. This overlook is about 6.5 miles from Height of Land. From here, continue east.

❺ Rangeley (p119)

An adventure hub, with tidy inns and down-home restaurants, Rangeley makes a useful base for skiing, hiking, white-water rafting and mountain biking in the nearby mountains. Snowmobilers can zoom across 150 miles of trails. For information, stop by the **Rangeley Lakes Chamber of Commerce** (☎207-864-5364; www.rangeleymaine.com; 6 Park Rd; ⏰10am-4pm Mon-Sat, plus noon-3pm Sun Jul & Aug), which

KENNETH H THOMAS/GETTY IMAGES ©

has handouts about restaurants, lodging options, local trails and moose watching. Just behind the visitor center, **Rangeley Lakes Park** (⏰5am-10pm) is a nice spot to enjoy a picnic by the lake. On rainy days ask at the chamber about the local museums.

The Drive » ME 4 breaks from ME 16 in downtown Rangeley. From the chamber of commerce, follow ME 4 east. Turn left onto Dallas Hill Rd, then in 2.5 miles bear right on Saddleback Mountain Rd and continue another 2.5 miles.

Mooselookmeguntic Lake

TRIP HIGHLIGHT

6 Rangeley Lakes Trails Center

A green yurt marks your arrival at the **Rangeley Lakes Trails Center** (☎207-864-4309; www. rangeleylakestrailscenter.com; 523 Saddleback Mountain Rd; day pass during snow season adult/child $18/10, rest of year by donation), a four-season trail system covering gorgeous woodland terrain beside Saddleback Lake. Here there are more than 34 miles of trails for cross-country skiing and snowshoeing during snow season. You can rent equipment inside the yurt. At other times the cross-country trails double as hiking trails, and the snowshoe trails allow single-track biking. The yurt is closed in summer, but trail maps are available at the adjacent information kiosk and the chamber of commerce. Visit the website for details about the hiking trails.

The Drive » Follow ME 4 southeast, passing another Rangeley Lake overlook. Continue southeast. You'll pass another Appalachian Trail crossing before entering prime moose country. Follow ME 12 east to ME 16/27 north.

7 Maine Huts & Trails Office

If you enjoy hiking and cross-country skiing, but not backpacking, consider a hut-to-hut trip through **Maine Huts & Trails** (☎877-634-8824; www.mainehuts. org; 496 Main St. Kingfield; r $79-199), a non-profit organization operating three overnight eco-lodges along a remote 45-mile trail near Sugarloaf. Choose a

HERE A MOOSE, THERE A MOOSE

Moose-crossing signs are as ubiquitous as logging trucks in these parts. But spotting one of these chunky beasts, which can reach a height of 7ft at the shoulder and weigh anywhere from 1000lb to 1400lb, is trickier. You'll most likely see them eating on the side of the road in the morning, in the evening and between noon and 2pm. According to a handout from the Rangeley Lakes Chamber of Commerce, these are some of the top moose-spotting sites in the area:

Route 4 Phillips to Rangeley (we saw one here in late April, early in the evening).

Route 16 Rangeley to Stratton; Wilsons Mills to the New Hampshire border.

Route 17 Between the Height of Land overlook and the Rangeley Lake overlook.

Route 16/27 Stratton to Carrabassett Valley.

When driving these routes stay extra vigilant and slow down, particularly at night. Moose don't always leap out of the way like deer do, and in the dark your vehicle's headlights won't always reflect off the animals' eyes, due to their height. If you come upon a moose standing in the road, do not get out of the car or drive around it (they may charge the vehicle). Wait for the moose to mosey off the road.

dorm bed or a private room and enjoy dinner, breakfast and a variety of room configurations. Pillows and blankets are provided, but not bedding. A second office and information center sits beside ME 16/27 in the Carrabassett Valley north of Kingfield. This trail-and-hut network is a work in progress; the plan is to extend the trail to 180 miles, with more huts along the way. The trail system is open to the public free of charge.

There is no vehicle access to the huts.

The Drive » From Kingfield, ME 16 joins ME 27, unfurling beneath the pines, with the Carrabassett River tumbling merrily alongside.

- - - - - - - - - - - - - -

8 Sugarloaf

Rangeley's most popular **ski resort** (📞207-237-2000; www.sugarloaf.com; 5092 Sugarloaf Access Rd, Carrabassett Valley; adult/child $79/55; 👪), Sugarloaf has a vertical drop of 2820ft, with 153 trails and glades

and 14 lifts. This is Maine's second-highest peak (4237ft). Out-of-season activities include lift rides, zip lines and golf. The resort village complex has an enormous mountain lodge, an inn and rental condos.

Near Sugarloaf's slopes, the **Sugarloaf Outdoor Center** (📞207-237-6830; www.sugarloaf.com/outdoorcenter; adult/child $20/12) has nearly 56 miles of groomed cross-country trails and an NHL-size skating rink.

Right View of Cascade Falls (p47) from ME 26

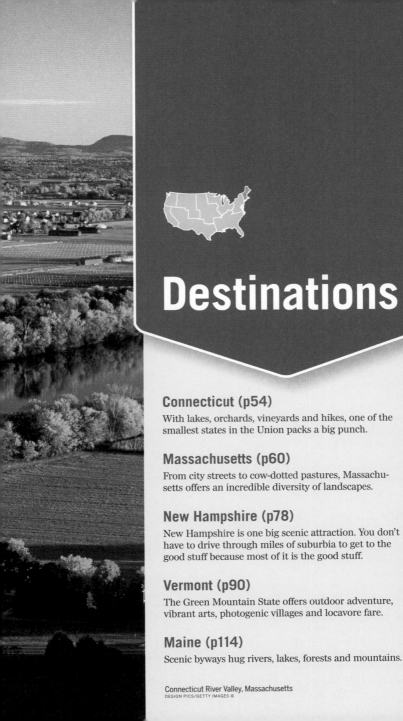

Destinations

Connecticut (p54)

With lakes, orchards, vineyards and hikes, one of the smallest states in the Union packs a big punch.

Massachusetts (p60)

From city streets to cow-dotted pastures, Massachusetts offers an incredible diversity of landscapes.

New Hampshire (p78)

New Hampshire is one big scenic attraction. You don't have to drive through miles of suburbia to get to the good stuff because most of it is the good stuff.

Vermont (p90)

The Green Mountain State offers outdoor adventure, vibrant arts, photogenic villages and locavore fare.

Maine (p114)

Scenic byways hug rivers, lakes, forests and mountains.

Connecticut River Valley, Massachusetts
DESIGN PICS/GETTY IMAGES ©

Connecticut

The Constitution State has long been luring artists, celebrities and moneyed Manhattanites, who appreciate the rural landscape sprinkled with small vineyards and genteel Colonial towns.

Sandwiched between sexy New York City and quainter quarters in northern New England, Connecticut often gets short shrift from travelers. But the Litchfield Hills, with lakes, vineyards and hiking trails capture Connecticut as it's been for centuries, while the pristine scenery of the Connecticut River Valley began luring artists in the 1900s and it's easy to see what inspired them.

History

The name 'Connecticut' comes from the Mohegan name for the great river that bisects the state. A number of Native American tribes (including the Mohegan, as well as the Pequot and others) were here when the first European explorers, primarily Dutch, appeared in the early 17th century. The first English settlement was at Old Saybrook in 1635, followed a year later by the Connecticut Colony, built by Massachusetts Puritans under Thomas Hooker. A third colony was founded in 1638 in New Haven. After the Pequot War (1637), the Native Americans were no longer a check to colonial expansion in New England, and Connecticut's English population grew. In 1686 Connecticut was brought into the Dominion of New England.

The American Revolution swept through Connecticut, with major battles leaving scars at Stonington (1775), Danbury (1777), New Haven (1779) and Groton (1781). Connecticut

---

CONNECTICUT LEAF-PEEPS

Kent has previously been voted *the* spot in all of New England for fall foliage viewing. But the fact is the whole of the densely wooded Housatonic River Valley offers numerous opportunities for leaf-peeping:

➡ **Squantz Pond** (p18) For shoreline walks with views of bristling mountains carpeted with forests plunging straight down to the pond.

➡ **Lake Waramaug** (p57) For fabulous foliage reflected in the mirrorlike lake.

➡ **Boyd Woods Audubon Sanctuary** (www.lhasct.org/www.lhasct.org/Boyd_Woods.html) For gentle walks through deciduous woodland alongside Wigwam Pond and milkweed meadow in Litchfield.

➡ **Kent Falls State Park** (p58) For a leaf-framed waterfall and Technicolor mountain views from Macedonia Brook State Park.

➡ **West Cornwall** (p59) For a covered bridge set against the tree-lined Housatonic River.

became the fifth state in 1788. It embarked on a period of prosperity, propelled by whaling, shipbuilding, farming and manufacturing (from firearms to bicycles to household tools), which lasted well into the 19th century.

The 20th century brought world wars and the Great Depression but, thanks in no small part to Connecticut's munitions industries, the state was able to fight back. Everything from planes to submarines was made in the state, and when the defense industry began to decline in the 1990s, the growth of other businesses (such as insurance) helped pick up the slack.

ℹ Information

There are welcome centers at the Hartford airport, and on I-95 and I-84 when entering the state by car.

Connecticut Tourism Division (www.ctvisit.com) Distributes visitor information for the entire state.

Hartford Courant (www.courant.com) The state's largest newspaper.

Hartford

Connecticut's capital city, Hartford has been lovingly dubbed the 'filing cabinet of America.' But this underappreciated city – one of the oldest in New England – harbors a rich cultural heritage. Besides being the former 'insurance capital' of America, it is also a former publishing center, which means that Hartford was home to some of the country's most celebrated writers. The **Greater Hartford Welcome Center** (☎860-244-0253; www.letsgoarts.org/welcomecenter; 100 Pearl St; ☻9am-5pm Mon-Fri) distributes tourist information.

Options for sleeping in Hartford are limited to national chain hotels.

◉ Sights

★ **Mark Twain House & Museum**　　MUSEUM
(www.marktwainhouse.org; 351 Farmington Ave; adult/child $19/11; ☻9:30am-5:30pm, closed Tue in Mar) It was at this former home of Samuel Langhorne Clemens, aka Mark Twain, that the legendary author penned many of his greatest works, including *The Adventures of Huckleberry Finn* and *Tom Sawyer*. The house itself, a Victorian Gothic with fanciful turrets and gables, reflects Twain's quirky character.

★ **Connecticut Science Center**　　MUSEUM
(www.ctsciencecenter.org; 250 Columbus Blvd; adult/child $22/15, movie $7/6; ☻10am-5pm; ℗) Designed by Italian architect César Pelli,

Mark Twain House
SEANPAVONEPHOTO/GETTY IMAGES ©

Connecticut's Science Center is both an exciting architectural space and an absorbing museum for adults and kids alike. Innovative, interactive exhibits and programs abound. There's a dedicated KidSpace on the 1st floor and a roster of fascinating temporary exhibitions.

You could easily spend a whole day here, but it's best to arrive after 2pm when the school groups clear out. In July the museum hosts a special barbecue evening during Riverfest which gets you a front row spot on the terrace for a fireworks display.

Teachers are eligible for significant discounts.

★ **Wadsworth Atheneum**　　MUSEUM
(www.thewadsworth.org; 600 Main St; adult/child $10/5; ☻11am-5pm Wed-Fri, 10am-5pm Sat & Sun) The nation's oldest public-art museum, the Wadsworth Atheneum houses nearly 50,000 pieces. On display are paintings by members of the Hudson River School, European Old Masters, 19th-century impressionist works, sculptures by Connecticut artist Alexander Calder, and a small yet outstanding array of surrealist works.

Harriet Beecher Stowe House　　MUSEUM
(www.harrietbeecherstowe.org; 77 Forest St; adult/child $10/7; ☻9:30am-5pm Tue-Sat, noon-5pm Sun) Next door to the Twain house is the house of the woman who wrote the anti-slavery book *Uncle Tom's Cabin*. It rallied so many Americans against slavery that

Hartford

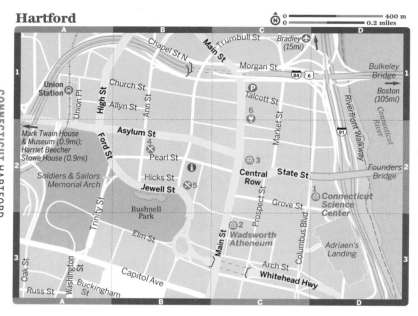

Hartford

Abraham Lincoln once credited Stowe with starting the US Civil War.

Old State House   HISTORIC BUILDING
(www.ctoldstatehouse.org; 800 Main St; adult/child $6/3; ⊙10am-5pm Tue-Sat Jul–mid-Oct, Mon-Fri mid-Oct–Jun; ⊕) Connecticut's original capitol building, designed by Charles Bulfinch, was the site of the trial of the *Amistad* prisoners. Gilbert Stuart's famous 1801 portrait of George Washington hangs in the senate chamber. Dedicated museum space houses interactive exhibits aimed at kids, as well as a **Museum of Curiosities** that features a two-headed calf, a narwhal's horn and a variety of mechanical devices.

✖ Eating & Drinking

Salute   ITALIAN $$
(☑860-899-1350; www.salutect.com; 100 Trumbull St; lunch mains $9-13, dinner $12-20; ⊙11:30am-11pm Mon-Thu, to midnight Fri-Sat, 3-10pm Sun; ✍) Charming service is the hallmark of this urban gem, which offers a contemporary take on Italian flavors. Regulars rave about the cheesy garlic bread, but there's plenty more on the menu that's worth trying. The pleasant patio overlooks Bushnell Park.

Bin 228   WINE BAR $$
(☑860-244-9463; www.bin228winebar.com; 228 Pearl St; panini & small plates $8-15; ⊙11:30am-10pm Mon-Thu, to midnight Fri, 4pm-midnight Sat) This wine bar serves Italian fare – panini, cheese platters, salads – alongside its expansive all-Italian wine list.

City Steam Brewery Café   BREWPUB
(www.citysteam.biz; 942 Main St; ⊙11:30am-1am Mon-Sat, 4-10pm Sun) This big and boisterous place has housemade beers on tap. The Naughty Nurse Pale Ale is a bestseller, and the seasonals are also worth a try. The brewery's basement is home to the **Brew Ha Ha Comedy Club** (tickets $10-15; ⊙Fri & Sat), where you can yuk it up with visiting comedians from New York and Boston.

Lake Candlewood

Lake Candlewood is the largest lake in Connecticut, and was created in the 1920s with water from the Housatonic River. The four towns of Brookfield, New Milford, Sherman and New Fairfield share Lake Candlewood's shoreline.

Stop in at White Silo Farm Winery (☑ 860-355-0271; www.whitesilowinery.com; 32 CT 37; tastings $7; ☺ 12-8pm Fri-Sun Apr-Dec; ⊕) for a unique tasting of wines made from farm-grown fruit. In September and October the fields are also open for blackberry and raspberry picking.

A local favorite, American Pie (www.americanpiecompany.com; 29 Sherman Rd/CT 37, Sherman; mains $9-20; ☺7am-9pm Tue-Sun, to 3pm Mon) serves up 20 varieties of homemade pie, including pumpkin and blueberry crumb, alongside burgers, steaks and salads.

Litchfield Hills

The rolling hills in the northwestern corner of Connecticut are sprinkled with lakes and carpeted with forests. Historic Litchfield is the hub of the region, but lesser-known villages such as Bethlehem, Kent, Lakeville and Norfolk are just as photogenic. The Western Connecticut Convention & Visitors Bureau (☑800-663-1273; www.litchfieldhills.com) has information on the region.

Litchfield

Founded in 1719, Litchfield prospered from the commerce brought by stagecoaches en route between Hartford and Albany, and its many handsome period buildings are a testimony to that era. A row of shops, restaurants and historic buildings overlooks the picturesque green. Stroll along North and South Sts to see the finest homes, including the 1773 Tapping Reeve House & Law School (www.litchfieldhistoricalsociety.org; 82 South St; adult/child $5/free; ☺11am-5pm Tue-Sat, 1-5pm Sun mid-Apr–Nov), the country's first law school.

Connecticut's largest wildlife preserve, the White Memorial Conservation Center (www.whitememorialcc.org; US 202; park free, museum adult/child $6/3; ☺park dawn-dusk, museum 9am-5pm Mon-Sat & noon-5pm Sun), 2 miles west of town, has 35 miles of walking trails and good bird-watching.

Lake Waramaug

The most beautiful of the dozens of lakes and ponds in the Litchfield Hills is Lake Waramaug. As you make your way around North Shore Rd, stop at Hopkins Vineyard (☑860-868-7954; www.hopkinsvineyard.com; 25 Hopkins Rd; ☺10am-5pm Mon-Sat & 11am-5pm Sun May-Dec, 10am-5pm Fri-Sun Jan-Feb, 10am-5pm Wed-Sun Mar-Apr) for wine tastings. The view from the bar is worth the trip, particularly when the foliage changes in the fall. Across the street, the 19th-century Hopkins Inn (☑860-868-7295; www.thehopkinsinn.com; 22 Hopkins Rd, Warren; r without/with bathroom from $125/135, apt $150; P✴☺) has lakeview accommodation and a recommended restaurant.

Bethlehem

Bethlehem is Connecticut's 'Christmas Town': every year thousands of visitors come for the Christmas Fair (www.christmastownfestival.com) and to have their Christmas mail hand-stamped in the village post office.

The town's religious history extends to the founding of the first theological seminary in America, by local resident Rev Joseph Bellamy. His home, the Bellamy-Ferriday House & Garden (☑203-266-7596; http://www.ci.bethlehem.ct.us/bellamy_ferriday.htm; 9 Main St North; adult/child $7/4; ☺noon-4pm Thu-Sun May-Sep, Sat & Sun Oct), a 1750s clapboard mansion, is a treasure trove of Delftware, Asian art and period furnishings. Equally exquisite is the garden, the creation of latter-day

---

LOCAL KNOWLEDGE

BANTAM CINEMA

Locals know that one of the best things to do on rainy days is book in to see a film at the Bantam Cinema (☑860-567-1916; www.bantamcinema.com; 115 Bantam Lake Rd, Bantam). Housed in a converted red barn on the shores of Lake Bantam, it's the oldest continuously operating movie theatre in Connecticut and is a real Litchfield experience. The well-curated screenings focus on independent and foreign films, and the 'Meet the Filmmaker' series features guest directors, actors and producers.

owner Caroline Ferriday, who designed it to resemble an Aubusson Persian carpet, its geometric box hedges infilled with peonies, lilacs and heirloom roses.

Bethlehem is also the location of one of the area's best restaurants, the quietly sophisticated Woodward House (☑203-266-6902; www.thewoodwardhouse.com; 4 The Green; meals $45-60; ◷5-9pm Wed-Sun), a 1740s saltbox with original wainscoting and hand-hewn beams, serving a modern American menu.

Kent

During summer and fall, weekenders (often arriving on Thursday) throng to Kent's small but respected clutch of art galleries and to its August Jazz Festival (www.litchfield-jazzfest.com). The small town on the banks of the Housatonic River is also a popular stop for hikers on the Appalachian Trail (www.appalachiantrail.org), which intersects CT 341 about 2 miles northwest of town. Unlike much of the trail, the Kent section offers a mostly flat 5-mile river walk alongside the Housatonic, the longest river walk along its entire length.

Two miles north of town, the quirky, Eric Sloane Museum & Kent Iron Furnace (☑860-927-3849; www.cultureandtourism.org; US 7; adult/child $3/1.50; ◷10am-4pm Thu-Sun May-Oct) is a barnful of early colonial tools and implements – some dating from the 17th century – collected and arranged by artist and author Eric Sloane, who painted the cloud-filled sky mural at the Smithsonian Air and Space Museum.

At Kent Falls State Park, about 5 miles north of town, the water drops 250ft over a quarter mile before joining up with the Housatonic River. Hike the easy trail to the top of the cascade, or just settle into a sunny picnic spot at the bottom near a red covered bridge. More extensive hiking trails (over 80 miles of them) can be found in Macedonia State Park (www.ct.gov/deep; 159 Macedonia Brook Rd; ◷mid-Apr–Sep; ⛺) cresting the rocky ridges of Cobble Mountain. The 51 camping sites (residents/nonresidents $14/24) here are much in demand in summer.

You can rent bikes at Bicycle Tour Company (☑888-711-5368; www.bicycletours.com; 9 Bridge St), or it can customize a guided ride for you around the area.

🛏 Sleeping & Eating

Inn at Kent Falls   HISTORIC INN $$$
(☑860-927-3197; www.theinnatkentfalls.com; 107 Kent-Cornwall Rd/US 7; r $215-350; P 🛜 🏊)
This historic inn dates back to the early 1900s. Original floorboards, three generous lounges with open fireplaces and a grand piano make for a home-away-from-home atmosphere. Breakfast is a communal affair with homemade pancakes and fresh baked croissants.

Gifford's   MODERN AMERICAN $$$
(☑860-592-0262; www.jpgifford.com; 9 Maple St; meals $20-35; ◷5-9pm Wed-Sat, 4-8pm Sun)
From Gifford's successful micromarket, bakery and deli to a new rousingly acclaimed restaurant on Maple St, Michael Moriarty and James Neunzig are definitely on the up. As you'd expect from experienced specialty provedores the secret is in the ingredients: meat from Mountain Products Smokehouse, golden-hued chicken from FreeBird and Connecticut-harvested clams. On top of that, the stylish contemporary interiors painted in sunshine blocks of color and the covered terrace make for a truly memorable dining experience.

CONNECTICUT FACTS

Nicknames Constitution State, Nutmeg State

Population 3.6 million

Area 4845 sq miles

Capital city Hartford (population 124,700)

Other cities New Haven (population 130,280)

Sales tax 6.35%

Birthplace of Abolitionist John Brown (1800–59), circus man PT Barnum (1810–91), actress Katharine Hepburn (1907–2003)

Home of The first written constitution in the US; the first lollipop, Frisbee and helicopter

Politics Democrat-leaning

Famous for Starting the US insurance biz and building the first nuclear submarine

Quirkiest state song lyrics 'Yankee Doodle', which entwines patriotism with doodles, feathers and macaroni

Driving distances Hartford to New Haven 40 miles; Hartford to Providence 75 miles

West Cornwall

The village of West Cornwall is just one of six Cornwall villages in Connecticut, but it is the most famous thanks to its picturesque covered bridge. The bridge was known as the 'Kissing Bridge,' because its long span allowed horse-drawn carriages to slow down inside it, allowing their passengers some complimentary canoodling.

Otherwise the area attracts nature lovers, birders and hikers who come to hike, fish and boat on the lazy Housatonic River. Housatonic Meadows State Park (☑860-927-3238; www.ct.gov/deep; US 7; ⊙8am-sunset) is famous for its 2-mile-long stretch of water set aside exclusively for fly-fishing. Its campground (☑860-672-6772; sites CT residents/nonresidents $17/27; ⊙mid-Apr–mid-Oct) has 97 sites on the banks of the Housatonic.

In winter the nearby Mohawk Mountain Ski Area (www.mohawkmtn.com; 42 Great Hollow Rd, Cornwall) is the largest ski resort in the state with 24 slopes and trails. On Labor Day weekend, in the nearby town of Goshen, you can visit the Goshen Fair (www.goshenfair.org), one of Connecticut's best old-fashioned fairs with ox-pulling and wood-cutting contests.

The tranquil, 14-room Cornwall Inn (☑860-672-6884; www.cornwallinn.com; 270 Kent Rd/US 7, Cornwall Bridge; r $159-199, ste incl breakfast $239-259; ⓟ🛜💹) offers rustic accommodation and a straightforward country breakfast.

Lakeville & Around

A quiet and remote corner of the Litchfield hills, the rolling farmland around Lakeville is home to millionaires and movie luminaries such as Meryl Streep. Motor races, including a series of vintage car races, take place at the venerable Lime Rock Race Track (www.limerock.com; 60 White Hollow Rd; ⊙Apr-Nov) from May to October. Paul Newman raced here and thought its seven-turn, 1.5 mile track the most beautiful racing track in America.

Nearby in teeny-tiny Falls Village you'll find the gorgeous Falls Village Inn (☑860-824-0033; www.thefallsvillageinn.com; 33 Railroad St; d/ste $209/299; ⓟ🛜), which originally served the Housatonic Railroad. Now the six rooms are styled by interior decorator Bunny Williams, and the Tap Room is a hangout for Lime Rock's racers.

Tea lovers will want to check out Mary O'Brien's shop Chaiwalla (☑860-435-9758;

Kent Falls State Park
SEANPAVONEPHOTO/GETTY IMAGES

1 Main St/US 44, Salisbury; items $3-10; ⊙10am-6pm Wed-Sun) in next-door Salisbury, which serves a variety of tea, especially unblended Darjeelings, as well as traditional accompaniments. Try Mary's famous tomato pie.

Norfolk

Norfolk's bucolic scenery and cool summers have long attracted prosperous New Yorkers. They built many of the town's fine mansions, its well-endowed Romanesque revival library and its arts-and-crafts–style town hall, now the Infinity Music Hall & Bistro (☑box office 866-666-6306; www.infinityhall.com; 20 Greenwoods Rd W; ⊙5-9pm Thu-Sun). This beautiful building with its original stage brings top acoustic, blues, jazz and folk acts to Norfolk from New York and beyond.

Opposite the Infinity is the opulent Whitehall, the summer estate of Ellen and Carl Battell Stoeckel, passionate and monied music lovers who established the Norfolk Chamber Music Festival (www.norfolkmusic.org; Ellen Battell Stoeckel Estate, US 44; tickets $25-100; ⊙Jul-Aug). These extravagant affairs – the couple brought the 70-piece New York Philharmonic orchestra to perform – were among the most popular summer events in New England. On her death, in 1939, Ellen Battell Stoeckel bequeathed the redwood 'Music Shed' to Yale University Summer School of Music, ensuring the tradition continues today.

From Boston's universities and museums to the woodsy hills of the Berkshires, Massachusetts is filled with opportunities to explore culture and the great outdoors.

Massachusetts

Boston

For all intents and purposes, Boston is the oldest city in America. And you can hardly walk a step over its cobblestone streets without running into some historic site. But Boston has not been relegated to the past. The city's art and music scenes continue to charm and challenge contemporary audiences; cutting-edge urban planning projects are reshaping the city; and scores of universities guarantee an infusion of cultural energy year after year.

History

When the Massachusetts Bay Colony was established by England in 1630, Boston became its capital. It's a city of firsts: Boston Latin School, the first public school in the USA, was founded in 1635, followed a year later by Harvard, the nation's first university. The first newspaper in the colonies was printed here in 1704, America's first labor union organized here in 1795 and the country's first subway system opened in Boston in 1897.

DON'T MISS

MASSACHUSETTS LEAF-PEEPS

....

Mohawk Trail (p41)
Mt Greylock State Reservation (p22)
Fall Foliage Parade (p22)

Not only were the first battles of the American Revolution fought nearby, but Boston was also home to the first African American regiment to fight in the US Civil War. Waves of immigrants, especially Irish in the mid-18th century and Italians in the early 20th, have infused the city with European influences.

◉ Sights

Boston's small size means that it's easy to walk and difficult to drive. Most of Boston's main attractions are found in or near the city center. Begin at Boston Common, where you'll find the tourist office and the start of the Freedom Trail.

Rising above Boston Common, Beacon Hill is one of the city's most historic and affluent neighborhoods. To the east is Downtown Boston, with a curious mix of Colonial sights and modern office buildings.

On the north side of the Charles River lies Cambridge, home to Harvard University and Massachusetts Institute of Technology (MIT). **Harvard Square** overflows with cafes, bookstores and street performers.

★**Boston Common**　　　　　PARK
(btwn Tremont, Charles, Beacon & Park Sts; ☺6am-midnight; [P] [♿]; [T] Park St) The Boston Common has served many purposes over the years, including as a campground for British troops during the Revolutionary War and as green grass for cattle grazing until 1830. The common today serves picnickers,

sunbathers and people-watchers. This is also the starting point for the Freedom Trail.

⭐ **Public Garden**   GARDENS
(www.friendsofthepublicgarden.org; Arlington St; ☺6am–midnight; 🚻; ⓣArlington) Adjoining Boston Common, the Public Garden is a 24-acre botanical oasis of Victorian flower beds, verdant grass and weeping willow trees shading a tranquil lagoon. The old-fashioned pedal-powered **Swan Boats** (www. swanboats.com; adult/child $3/1.50; ☺10am-5pm Jun-Aug, to 4pm mid-Apr–May, noon-4pm Sep; ⓣArlington) have been delighting children for generations. The most endearing statue in the Public Garden is *Make Way for Ducklings,* depicting Mrs Mallard and her eight ducklings, the main characters in the beloved book by Robert McCloskey.

Old State House   HISTORIC BUILDING
(www.revolutionaryboston.org; 206 Washington St; adult/child $10/free; ☺9am-6pm Jun-Aug, to 5pm Sep-May; ⓣState) Dating to 1713 the Old State House is Boston's oldest surviving public building. The building is best known for its balcony, where the Declaration of Independence was first read to Bostonians in 1776. Inside, the Old State House contains a small museum of revolutionary memorabilia, with multimedia presentations about the Boston Massacre, which took place out front.

⭐ **New England Aquarium**   AQUARIUM
(www.neaq.org; Central Wharf; adult/child $25/18; ☺9am-5pm Mon-Fri, to 6pm Sat & Sun, 1hr later Jul & Aug; 🅿🚻; ⓣAquarium) 🏊 Teeming with sea creatures of all sizes, shapes and colors, this giant fishbowl is the centerpiece of Downtown Boston's waterfront. The main attraction is the three-story Giant Ocean Tank, which swirls with thousands of creatures great and small, including turtles, sharks and eels. Countless side exhibits explore the lives and habitats of other underwater oddities, as well as penguins and marine mammals.

⭐ **Boston Tea Party Ships & Museum**   MUSEUM
(www.bostonteapartyship.com; Congress St Bridge; adult/child $25/15; ☺10am-5pm, last tour 4pm; 🚻; ⓣSouth Station) To protest unfair taxes, a gang of rebellious colonists dumped 342 chests of tea into the water. The 1773 protest – the Boston Tea Party – set into motion the events leading to the Revolutionary War. Nowadays replica Tea Party Ships are moored at the reconstructed Griffin's Wharf, alongside an excellent experiential museum.

MASSACHUSETTS FACTS
....

Nickname Bay State

Population 6.7 million

Area 7840 sq miles

Capital city Boston (population 646,000)

Other cities Worcester (population 182,500), Springfield (population 153,700)

Sales tax 6.25%

Birthplace of Inventor Benjamin Franklin (1706–90), John F Kennedy (1917–63), and authors Jack Kerouac (1922–69) and Henry David Thoreau (1817–62)

Home of Harvard University, Boston Marathon, Plymouth Rock

Politics Democratic

Famous for Boston Tea Party; first state to legalize gay marriage

Driving distances Boston to the Berkshires 130 miles; Boston to Northampton 104 miles; Boston to Springfield 92 miles

State Sweets Boston Cream Pie, Dunkin' Donuts, Fig Newtons

⭐ **Boston Public Library**   LIBRARY
(www.bpl.org; 700 Boylston St; ☺9am-9pm Mon-Thu, to 5pm Fri & Sat year-round, also 1-5pm Sun Oct-May; ⓣCopley) Dating from 1852 the esteemed Boston Public Library lends credence to Boston's reputation as the 'Athens of America.' The old McKim Building is notable for its magnificent facade and exquisite interior art. Pick up a free brochure and take a self-guided tour; alternatively, free guided tours depart from the entrance hall (times vary).

⭐ **Trinity Church**   CHURCH
(www.trinitychurchboston.org; 206 Clarendon St; adult/child $7/free; ☺9am-4:30pm Mon, Fri & Sat, to 5:30pm Tue-Thu, 1-5pm Sun; ⓣCopley) A masterpiece of American architecture, Trinity Church is the country's ultimate example of Richardsonian Romanesque. The granite exterior, with a massive portico and side cloister, uses sandstone in colorful patterns. The interior is an awe-striking array of vibrant murals and stained glass, most by artist John LaFarge, who cooperated closely with architect Henry Hobson Richardson to create an integrated composition of shapes, colors and textures. Free architectural tours are offered following Sunday service at 11:15am.

Central Boston

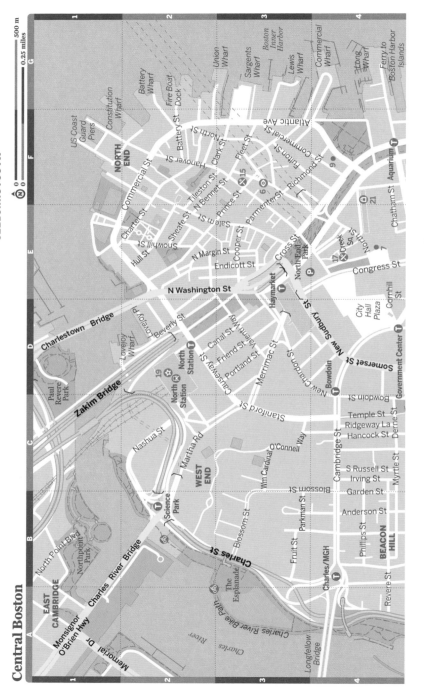

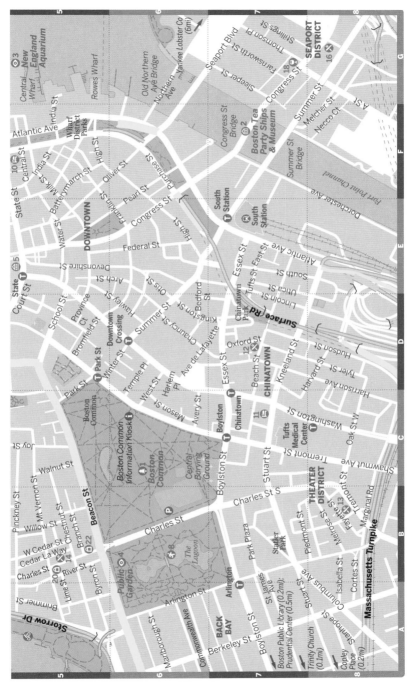

63

Central Boston

MASSACHUSETTS BOSTON

Paul Revere House HISTORIC SITE
(www.paulreverehouse.org; 19 North Sq; adult/child $3.50/1; ⊙9:30am-5:15pm mid-Apr–Oct, to 4:15pm Nov–mid-Apr, closed Mon Jan-Mar; ⊞; Ⓣ Haymarket) When silversmith Paul Revere rode to warn patriots of the British march to Lexington and Concord, he set out from his home on North Sq. This small clapboard house was built in 1680, making it the oldest house in Boston. A self-guided tour through the house and courtyard gives visitors a glimpse of what everyday life was like for the Revere family.

Prudential Center Skywalk Observatory LOOKOUT
(www.skywalkboston.com; 800 Boylston St; adult/child $16/11; ⊙10am-10pm Mar-Oct, to 8pm Nov-Feb; ⊞⊞; Ⓣ Prudential) Technically called the Shops at Prudential Center, this landmark Boston building is not much more than a fancy shopping mall. But it does provide a bird's-eye view of Boston from its 50th-floor skywalk. Completely enclosed by glass, the skywalk offers spectacular 360-degree views of Boston and Cambridge, accompanied by an entertaining audio tour (with a special version catering to kids). Alternatively, enjoy the same view from **Top of the Hub** (☑617-536-1775; www.topofthehub.net; 800 Boylston St; ⊙11:30am-1am; ☎; Ⓣ Prudential) for the price of a drink.

★ Museum of Fine Arts MUSEUM
(MFA; www.mfa.org; 465 Huntington Ave; adult/child $25/10; ⊙10am-10pm Sat-Tue, to 10pm Wed-Fri; ⊞; Ⓣ Museum or Ruggles) Since 1876 the Museum of Fine Arts has been Boston's premier venue for showcasing art by local, national and international artists. Nowadays, the museum's holdings encompass all eras, from the ancient world to contemporary times, and all areas of the globe, making it truly encyclopedic in scope. Most recently, the museum has added gorgeous new wings dedicated to the art of the Americas and to contemporary art, contributing to Boston's emergence as an art center in the 21st century.

★ Harvard University UNIVERSITY
(www.harvard.edu; Massachusetts Ave; tours free; ⊙tours hourly 10am-3pm Mon-Sat; Ⓣ Harvard) Founded in 1636 to educate men for the ministry, Harvard is America's oldest college. The original Ivy League school has eight graduates who went on to be US presidents, not to mention dozens of Nobel laureates and Pulitzer Prize winners. It educates 6500 undergraduates and about 12,000 graduates yearly in 10 professional schools. The geographic heart of Harvard University – where redbrick buildings and leaf-covered paths exude academia – is Harvard Yard.

★ Isabella Stewart Gardner Museum MUSEUM
(www.gardnermuseum.org; 280 The Fenway; adult/child $15/free; ⊙11am-5pm Mon, Wed & Fri-Sun, to 9pm Thu; ⊞; Ⓣ Museum) The magnificent Venetian-style palazzo that houses this museum was home to 'Mrs Jack' Gardner herself until her death in 1924. A monument to one woman's taste for acquiring exquisite art, the Gardner is filled with almost 2000 priceless objects, primarily European, including outstanding tapestries, and Italian Renaissance and 17th-century Dutch paintings. The four-story greenhouse courtyard is a masterpiece and a tranquil oasis that alone is worth the price of admission.

★ Harvard Art Museums   MUSEUM
(www.harvardartmuseums.org; 32 Quincy St; adult/child $15/free; ⏱10am-5pm; Ⓣ Harvard) Architect extraordinaire Renzo Piano has overseen a renovation and expansion of Harvard's art museums, allowing the university's massive 250,000-piece collection to come together under one very stylish roof. Harvard's art spans the globe, with separate collections devoted to Asian and Islamic cultures (formerly the Arthur M Sackler Museum), Northern European and Germanic cultures (formerly the Busch-Reisinger Museum) and other Western art, especially European modernism (formerly the Fogg).

☞ Tours

★ Urban AdvenTours   BICYCLE TOUR
(⏱617-379-3590; www.urbanadventours.com; 103 Atlantic Ave; tours $55; ⏰; Ⓣ Aquarium) ✈ Founded by avid cyclists who believe the best views of Boston are from a bicycle. The City View Ride provides a great overview of how to get around by bike, and there are other specialty tours such as Bikes at Night and the Emerald Necklace tour.

Boston by Foot   WALKING TOUR
(www.bostonbyfoot.com; adult/child $15/10; ⏰) This fantastic nonprofit offers 90-minute walking tours, with neighborhood-specific walks and specialty theme tours such as Literary Landmarks, the Dark Side of Boston and Boston for Little Feet – a kid-friendly version of the Freedom Trail.

NPS Freedom Trail Tour   WALKING TOUR
(www.nps.gov/bost; Faneuil Hall; ⏱10am & 2pm Apr-Oct; Ⓣ State) FREE Show up at least 30 minutes early to snag a spot on one of the free, ranger-led Freedom Trail tours provided by the NPS. Tours depart from the visitor center in Faneuil Hall, and follow a portion of the Freedom Trail (not including Charlestown), for a total of 90 minutes.

🛏 Sleeping

Boston has high hotel prices, but online discounts can lessen the sting at even high-end places. You'll typically find the best deals on weekends. Try also Bed & Breakfast Associates Bay Colony (⏱888-486-6018, 617-720-0522; www.bnbboston.com), which handles B&Bs, rooms and apartments.

HI-Boston   HOSTEL $
(⏱617-536-9455; www.bostonhostel.org; 19 Stuart St; dm $55-65, d $199; ✳@⏰; Ⓣ Chinatown or Boylston) ✈ HI-Boston sets the standard for urban hostels, with its new, ecofriendly facility in the historic Dill Building. Purpose-built rooms are comfortable and clean, as are the shared bathrooms. Community spaces are numerous, from the fully equipped kitchen to a trendy ground-floor cafe, and there's a whole calendar of activities on offer. The place is large, but it books out, so reserve in advance.

40 Berkeley   HOSTEL $$
(⏱617-375-2524; www.40berkeley.com; 40 Berkeley St; s/d/tr/q from $95/103/121/130; ⏰; Ⓣ Back Bay) Straddling the South End and Back Bay, this safe, friendly hostelry was the first YWCA in the country. It's no longer a Y, but it still rents some 200 basic rooms (some overlooking the lovely garden) to guests on a nightly and long-term basis. Bathrooms are shared, as are other useful facilities including telephone, library, TV room and laundry.

Newbury Guest House   GUESTHOUSE $$
(⏱617-437-7666, 617-437-7668; www.newbury guesthouse.com; 261 Newbury St; d from $209; Ⓟ✳⏰; Ⓣ Hynes or Copley) Dating to 1882, these three interconnected brick and brownstone buildings offer a prime location in the heart of Newbury St. A recent renovation has preserved charming features such as ceiling medallions and in-room fireplaces, but now the rooms feature clean lines, luxurious linens and modern amenities. Each morning a complimentary continental breakfast is laid out next to the marble fireplace in the salon.

Oasis Guest House
& Adams B&B   GUESTHOUSE $$
(⏱617-230-0105, 617-267-2262; www.oasisguest house.com; 22 Edgerly Rd; s/d without bathroom $109/149, r with bathroom from $189; Ⓟ✳⏰; Ⓣ Hynes or Symphony) These homey side-by-side (jointly managed) guesthouses offer a peaceful, pleasant oasis in the midst of Boston's chaotic city streets. Thirty-odd guest

---

BOSTON IN TWO DAYS

Spend one day reliving Revolutionary history by following the **Freedom Trail**. Take time to lounge on the **Boston Common**, peek in the **Old State House** and imbibe a little history at the **Union Oyster House**. Afterwards, stroll into the **North End** for an Italian dinner. On your second day, rent a bike and ride along the Charles River. Go as far as **Harvard Sq** to cruise the campus and browse the bookstores.

City Walk
Freedom Trail

START BOSTON COMMON
FINISH BUNKER HILL MONUMENT
LENGTH 2.5 MILES; THREE HOURS

Trace America's earliest history along the Freedom Trail, which covers Boston's key Revolutionary sites. The well-trodden route is marked by a double row of red bricks, starting at the **1 Boston Common** (p60), America's oldest public park. Follow the trail north to the gold-domed **2 State House**, designed by Charles Bulfinch, America's first homegrown architect. Rounding Park St takes you past the Colonial-era **3 Park Street Church**; the **4 Granary Burying Ground**, which is the final resting place of many of your favorite revolutionary heroes; and **5 King's Chapel**, topped with one of Paul Revere's bells. Continue down School St, past the site of **6 Boston's first public school** and the **7 Old Corner Bookstore**, a haunt of 19th-century literati.

Nearby the **8 Old South Meeting House** tells the backstory of the Boston Tea Party. There are more Revolutionary exhibits at the **9 Old State House** (p61). Outside, a ring of cobblestones at the intersection marks the **10 Boston Massacre Site**, the first violent conflict of the American Revolution. Next up is **11 Faneuil Hall**, a public market since Colonial times.

Cross the Greenway to Hanover St, the main artery of the North End. Treat yourself to lunch before continuing to North Sq, where you can tour **12 Paul Revere House** (p64), the Revolutionary hero's former home. Follow the trail to the **13 Old North Church**, where a lookout in the steeple signaled to Revere that the British were coming, setting off his famous midnight gallop.

Walk northwest on Hull St, where you'll find more Colonial graves at **14 Copp's Hill Burying Ground**. Then cross the Charlestown Bridge to reach the **15 USS Constitution**, the world's oldest commissioned warship. To the north lies the **16 Bunker Hill Monument**, the site of the first battle fought in the American Revolution.

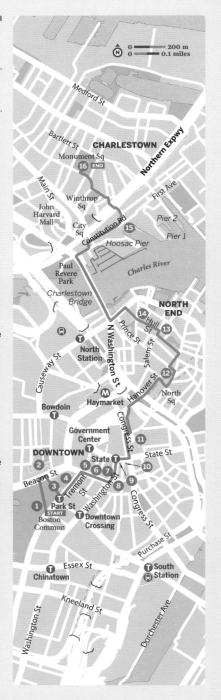

rooms occupy four attractive brick, bow-front town houses on this tree-lined lane. The modest, light-filled rooms are tastefully and traditionally decorated, most with queen beds, floral quilts and nondescript prints.

Verb Hotel
BOUTIQUE HOTEL $$$

(☏855-695-6678; www.theverbhotel.com; 1271 Boylston St; r from $250; P✳🐾🏊🐾; TKenmore) This former HoJo property is now Boston's most radical, retro, and rock and roll hotel. The style is mid-century modern; the theme is music. Memorabilia is on display throughout the joint, and a jukebox cranks out tunes in the lobby. Classy, clean-lined rooms face the swimming pool or Fenway Park. A+ for service and style.

Harborside Inn
BOUTIQUE HOTEL $$$

(☏617-723-7500; www.harborsideinnboston.com; 185 State St; r from $269; P✳@🐾; TAquarium) Steps from Faneuil Hall and the waterfront, this boutique hotel inhabits a respectfully renovated 19th-century mercantile warehouse. The 116 rooms are on the small side, but comfortable and appropriately nautically themed. Note that Atrium Rooms face the atrium (ahem) and Cabin Rooms have no windows at all. Add $20 for a city view (worth it).

Old State House (p61)
STEVE DUNWELL/GETTY IMAGES ©

Eating

New England cuisine is known for summertime clambakes and Thanksgiving turkey. But the Boston dining scene changes it up with wide-ranging international influences and contemporary interpretations. Indulge in affordable Asian fare in Chinatown and Italian feasts in the North End; or head to the South End for the city's trendiest foodie scene.

Gourmet Dumpling House
CHINESE, TAIWANESE $

(52 Beach St; dumplings $2-8, mains $10-15; ⊙11am-1am; ✐; TChinatown) *Xiao long bao*. That's all the Chinese you need to know to take advantage of the specialty at the Gourmet Dumpling House (or GDH, as it is fondly called). They are Shanghai soup dumplings, of course, and they are fresh, doughy and delicious. The menu offers plenty of other options, including scrumptious crispy scallion pancakes. Come early or be prepared to wait.

Yankee Lobster Co
SEAFOOD $

(www.yankeelobstercompany.com; 300 Northern Ave; mains $11-20; ⊙10am-9pm Mon-Sat, 11am-6pm Sun; 🚌SL1 or SL2, TSouth Station) The Zanti family have been fishing for three generations,

so they definitely know their stuff. A relatively recent addition is this retail fish market, scattered with a few tables in case you want to dine in. And you do. Order something simple such as clam chowder or a lobster roll and you will not be disappointed.

Clover Food Lab
VEGETARIAN $

(www.cloverfoodlab.com; 7 Holyoke St; mains $6-7; ⊙7am-midnight Mon-Sat, to 7pm Sun; 🐾✐; THarvard) 🍃 Clover is on the cutting edge. It's all high-tech with its 'live' menu updates and electronic ordering system. But it's really about the food – local, seasonal, vegetarian food – which is cheap, delicious and fast. How fast? Check the menu. Interesting tidbit: Clover started as a food truck (and still has a few trucks making the rounds).

Mike & Patty's
SANDWICHES $

(www.mikeandpattys.com; 12 Church St; sandwiches $7-9; ⊙7:30am-2pm Wed-Sun; ✐; TNew England Medical Center or Arlington) Tucked away in Bay Village, this tiny gem of a corner sandwich shop does amazing things between two slices of bread. There are only eight options and they're all pretty perfect, but the hands-down favorite is the Fancy (fried egg, cheddar cheese, bacon and avocado on multigrain).

Paramount
CAFETERIA $$

(www.paramountboston.com; 44 Charles St; mains breakfast & lunch $6-12, dinner $15-23; ⊙7am-10pm Mon-Thu, to 11pm Fri, 8am-11pm Sat, to 10pm Sun; ✐; TCharles/MGH) This old-fashioned cafeteria is a neighborhood favorite. A-plus diner fare includes pancakes, home fries, burgers and sandwiches, and big, hearty salads. Banana and caramel French toast is an obvious go-to for the brunch crowd. Don't sit down until you get your food! At dinner, add table service and candlelight, and the place goes upscale without losing its down-home charm.

Pomodoro
ITALIAN **$$**

(☑617-367-4348; 351 Hanover St; mains brunch $12, dinner $23-24; ⏱5-11pm Mon-Fri, noon-11pm Sat & Sun; Ⓣ Haymarket) Pomodoro has a new (only slightly larger) location, but it's still one of the North End's most romantic settings for delectable Italian. The food is simple but perfectly prepared: fresh pasta, spicy tomato sauce, grilled fish and meats, and wine by the glass. If you're lucky, you might be on the receiving end of a complimentary tiramisu for dessert. Cash only.

Row 34
SEAFOOD **$$**

(☑617-553-5900; www.row34.com; 383 Congress St; oysters $2-3, mains lunch $13-18, dinner $21-28; ⏱11:30am-10pm Mon-Fri, 5-10pm Sat & Sun; Ⓣ South Station) In the heart of the new Seaport District, this is a 'workingman's oyster bar' (by working man, they mean yuppie). Set in a sharp, postindustrial space, the place offers a dozen types of raw oysters and clams, alongside an amazing selection of craft beers. There's also a full menu of cooked seafood, ranging from the traditional to the trendy.

Courtyard
MODERN AMERICAN **$$**

(www.thecateredaffair.com; 700 Boylston St; mains $17-22; ⏱11:30am-4pm Mon-Fri; ✉; Ⓣ Copley) The perfect destination for an elegant luncheon with artfully prepared food is – believe it or not – the Boston Public Library. Overlooking the beautiful Italianate courtyard, this grown-up restaurant serves seasonal, innovative and exotic dishes (along with a few standards). After 2pm, the Courtyard serves a delightful afternoon tea ($32), with a selection of sandwiches, scones and sweets.

Myers & Chang
ASIAN **$$**

(☑617-542-5200; www.myersandchang.com; 1145 Washington St; small plates $10-18; ⏱11:30am-10pm Sun-Thu, to 11pm Fri & Sat; ✉; 🚌 SL4 or SL5, Ⓣ New England Medical Center) This super-hip Asian spot blends Thai, Chinese and Vietnamese cuisines, which means delicious dumplings, spicy stir-fries and oodles of noodles. The kitchen staff does amazing things with a wok, and the menu of small plates allows you to sample a wide selection of dishes. The vibe is casual but cool, international and original.

Island Creek Oyster Bar
SEAFOOD **$$$**

(☑617-532-5300; www.islandcreekoysterbar.com; 500 Commonwealth Ave; oysters $2.50-4, mains lunch $18-21, dinner $25-35; ⏱4pm-1am; Ⓣ Kenmore) Island Creek has united 'farmer, chef and diner in one space' – and what a space it is. ICOB serves up the region's finest oysters, along with other local seafood, in an ethereal new-age setting. The specialty – lobster roe noodles topped with braised short ribs and grilled lobster – lives up to the hype.

Union Oyster House
SEAFOOD **$$$**

(www.unionoysterhouse.com; 41 Union St; mains lunch $15-20, dinner $22-32; ⏱11am-9:30pm; Ⓣ Haymarket) The oldest restaurant in Boston, ye olde Union Oyster House has been serving seafood in this historic redbrick building since 1826. Countless history-makers have propped themselves up at this bar, including Daniel Webster and John F Kennedy. (Apparently JFK used to order the lobster bisque.) Overpriced but atmospheric.

Drinking & Nightlife

Bleacher Bar
SPORTS BAR

(www.bleacherbarboston.com; 82a Lansdowne St; ⏱11am-1am Sun-Wed, to 2am Thu-Sat; Ⓣ Kenmore) Tucked under the bleachers at Fenway Park, this classy bar offers a view onto center field. It's not the best place to watch the game, as the place gets packed, but it's a fun way to experience America's oldest ballpark, even when the Sox are not playing. Gentlemen: enjoy the view from the loo!

SEAFOOD SPECIALTIES

Lobster The mighty crustacean, steamed, and usually served in its shell

Lobster roll The succulent meat of the tail and claws, mixed with a touch of mayo and served on a grilled hot-dog bun

Clam chowder Or, as Bostonians say, *chow-dah*, combines chopped clams, potatoes and clam juice in a milk base

Oysters Usually served raw on the half-shell, with cocktail sauce and lemon

Steamers Soft-shelled clams, steamed and served in a bucket of briny broth

If you want a seat in front of the window, get your name on the waiting list an hour or two before game time; once seated, diners have 45 minutes in the hot seat.

Drink   COCKTAIL BAR
(www.drinkfortpoint.com; 348 Congress St; ⊙4pm-1am; 🚇SL1 or SL2, ⓣSouth Station) There is no cocktail menu at Drink. Instead you have a little chat with the bartender, and he or she will whip something up according to your specifications. The bar takes seriously the art of drink mixology – and you will too, after you sample one of its concoctions. The subterranean space creates a dark, sexy atmosphere, which makes for a great date destination.

☆ Entertainment

For up-to-the-minute listings, grab a copy of the free *Boston Phoenix*.

Club Passim   LIVE MUSIC
(📱617-492-7679; www.clubpassim.org; 47 Palmer St; tickets $15-30; ⓣHarvard) Folk music in Boston seems to be endangered outside of Irish bars, but legendary Club Passim does such a great job booking top-notch acts that it practically fills in the vacuum by itself. The colorful, intimate room is hidden off a side street in Harvard Sq, as it has been since 1969.

Boston Symphony Orchestra   CLASSICAL MUSIC
(BSO; 📱617-266-1200; www.bso.org; 301 Massachusetts Ave; tickets $30-115; ⓣSymphony) From September to April, the world-renowned Boston Symphony Orchestra performs in the beauteous **Symphony Hall** (www.bso.org; 301 Massachusetts Ave; ⊙tours 4pm Wed & 2pm Sat, reservations required), featuring an ornamental high-relief ceiling and attracting a fancy-dress crowd. Flawless acoustics match the BSO's ambitious programs.

TD Garden   BASKETBALL, ICE HOCKEY
(📱information 617-523-3030, tickets 617-931-2000; www.tdgarden.com; 150 Causeway St; ⓣNorth Station) The TD Garden is home to the Bruins, who play hockey here from September to June, and the Celtics, who play basketball from October to April.

🛍 Shopping

Newbury St in the Back Bay and Charles St on Beacon Hill are Boston's best shopping destinations for the biggest selection of shops, both traditional and trendy. Harvard Sq is famous for bookstores and the South End is the city's up-and-coming art district.
Copley Place (www.simon.com; 100 Huntington

Ave; ⊙10am-8pm Mon-Sat, noon-6pm Sun; ⓣBack Bay) and the **Prudential Center** (www.prudentialcenter.com; 800 Boylston St; ⊙10am-9pm Mon-Sat, 11am-8pm Sun; 📶; ⓣPrudential), both in Back Bay, are big indoor malls.

Ruby Door   JEWELRY
(www.therubydoor.com; 15 Charles St; ⊙11am-6pm Mon-Sat; ⓣCharles/MGH) What will you find behind the ruby door? Gorgeous, handcrafted jewelry, much of it featuring intriguing gemstones and unique vintage elements. Designer and owner Tracy Chareas reworks antique and vintage jewels into thoroughly modern pieces of art. There is also plenty of more affordable jewelry for bauble lovers. Great for browsing, with no pressure to buy.

Blackstone's of Beacon Hill   GIFTS, ACCESSORIES
(www.blackstonesbeaconhill.com; 46 Charles St; ⊙10am-6:30pm Mon-Sat, 11am-5pm Sun; ⓣCharles/MGH) Here's a guarantee: you will find the perfect gift for that certain someone at Blackstone's. This little place is crammed with classy, clever and otherwise unusual items. Highlights include the custom-designed stationery, locally made handicrafts and quirky Boston-themed souvenirs such as clocks and coasters.

Lucy's League   CLOTHING
(www.rosterstores.com/lucysleague; North Market, Faneuil Hall; ⊙10am-9pm Mon-Sat, to 6pm Sun; ⓣGovernment Center) We're not advocating those pink Red Sox caps, but sometimes a girl wants to look good while she's supporting the team. At Lucy's League, fashionable sports fans will find shirts, jackets and other gear sporting the local teams' logos in super-cute styles designed to flatter the female figure.

Converse   SHOES, CLOTHING
(www.converse.com; 348 Newbury St; ⊘10am-7pm Mon-Fri, to 8pm Sat, 11am-6pm Sun; ⓣHynes) Converse started making shoes right up the road in Malden, MA, way back in 1908. Chuck Taylor joined the 'team' in the 1920s and the rest is history. This retail store (one of three in the country) carries sneakers, denim and other gear. The iconic shoes come in all colors and patterns; make them uniquely your own at the in-store customization area.

❶ Information

INTERNET ACCESS

Aside from hotels, wireless access is common at cafes, on buses and even in public spaces like Faneuil Hall and the Greenway. Many cafes charge a fee, but may offer the first hour free of charge.

Boston Public Library (www.bpl.org; 700 Boylston St; ⊘9am-9pm Mon-Thu, to 5pm Fri & Sat year-round, 1-5pm Sun Oct-May; 🛜; ⓣCopley) Internet access free for 15-minute intervals. Or get a visitor courtesy card at the circulation desk and sign up for one hour of free terminal time. Arrive first thing in the morning to avoid long waits.

Wired Puppy (www.wiredpuppy.com; 250 Newbury St; ⊘6:30am-7:30pm; 🛜; ⓣHynes) Free wireless access and free computer use in case you don't have your own. This is also a comfortable, cozy place to just come and drink coffee.

TOURIST INFORMATION

Cambridge Visitor Information Kiosk (www.cambridge-usa.org; Harvard Sq; ⊘9am-5pm Mon-Fri, 1-5pm Sat & Sun; ⓣHarvard) Detailed information on current Cambridge happenings and self-guided walking tours.

Boston Common Information Kiosk (GBCVB Visitors Center; www.bostonusa.com; Boston Common; ⊘8:30am-5pm; ⓣPark St) Starting point for the Freedom Trail and many other walking tours.

USEFUL WEBSITES

My Secret Boston (www.mysecretboston.com) Not-that-secret restaurants, nightlife, cultural and family events.

Universal Hub (www.universalhub.com) Round-up of local news, with rich local commentary.

City of Boston (www.cityofboston.gov) Official city website with links to visitor services.

❶ Getting Around

Driving in Boston is not for the faint of heart. It's easier to get around the city on public transportation.

Parking in Downtown Boston is prohibitively expensive. For more affordable rates, cross the Fort Point Channel and park in the Seaport District

lots for a flat rate of $18; the Necco Street Garage (off A St) is only $5 on weekends..

Central Massachusetts

Poking around this central swath of Massachusetts, between big-city Boston and the fashionable Berkshires, provides a taste of the less-touristed stretch of the state. But it's no sleeper, thanks largely to a score of colleges which infuse a youthful spirit to the region.

The **Central Massachusetts Convention & Visitors Bureau** (☑508-755-7400; www.centralmass.org; 91 Prescott St, Worcester; ⊘9am-5pm Mon-Fri) and the **Greater Springfield Convention & Visitors Bureau** (☑413-787-1548; www.valleyvisitor.com; 1441 Main St, Springfield; ⊘8:30am-5pm Mon-Fri) provide regional information.

Springfield

Workaday Springfield gave birth to two American cultural icons, both of which are memorialized here.

★**Naismith Memorial Basketball Hall of Fame**   MUSEUM
(www.hoophall.com; 1000 W Columbus Ave; adult/child $22/15; ⊘10am-5pm; P ♿) Basketball devotees will be thrilled to measure their hoop skills against those of the game's greatest players, feel the center-court excitement and learn about the sport's history and origins.

Dr Seuss National Memorial Sculpture Garden   PARK
(www.catinthehat.org; 21 Edwards St; ⊘dawn-dusk; ♿) FREE Life-size bronze sculptures of the Cat in the Hat and other wonky characters look beseechingly at passers-by. Oh me, oh my. Welcome to the world of Theodor Seuss Geisel, Springfield's favorite native son.

Northampton

The region's best dining, hottest nightlife and most interesting street scenes all await in this uber-hip burg known for its liberal politics and outspoken lesbian community. Easy to explore on foot, the eclectic town center is chockablock with cafes, funky shops and art galleries. **Greater Northampton Chamber of Commerce** (☑413-584-1900; www.explorenorthampton.com; 99 Pleasant St; ⊘9am-5pm Mon-Fri year-round, 10am-2pm Sat & Sun May-Oct) is information central.

Sights

Smith College — COLLEGE CAMPUS
(www.smith.edu; Elm St; P) Founded 'for the education of the intelligent gentlewoman' in 1875, Smith College is one of the largest women's colleges in the country, with 2600 students. The verdant 125-acre campus holds an eclectic architectural mix of nearly 100 buildings and a pretty pond.

Smith College Museum of Art — MUSEUM
(www.smith.edu/artmuseum; Elm St at Bedford Tce; adult/child $5/2; ⏱10am-4pm Tue-Sat, noon-4pm Sun; P) This impressive campus museum boasts a 25,000-piece collection which is particularly strong in 17th-century Dutch and 19th- and 20th-century European and North American paintings, including works by Degas, Winslow Homer, Picasso and James Abbott McNeill Whistler.

Sleeping

Autumn Inn — MOTEL $$
(☏413-584-7660; www.hampshirehospitality. com; 259 Elm St/MA 9; r incl breakfast $119-179; P @ 🛜 🏊) Despite the motel layout, this two-story place near Smith campus has an agreeable ambience and large, comfy rooms.

Hotel Northampton — HISTORIC HOTEL $$
(☏413-584-3100; www.hotelnorthampton.com; 36 King St; r $185-275; P 🛜) Northampton's finest sleep since 1927, the 100-room hotel in the town center features period decor and well-appointed rooms.

Eating

Haymarket Café — CAFE $
(☏413-586-9969; www.haymarketcafe.com; 185 Main St; items $5-10; ⏱7am-10pm; 🛜 🍴) Northampton's coolest (and perhaps longest-standing) hangout for bohemians and caffeine addicts, the Haymarket serves up heady espresso, fresh juices and an extensive vegetarian menu.

Paul & Elizabeth's — SEAFOOD $$
(☏413-584-4832; www.paulandelizabeths.com; 150 Main St; mains $13-17; ⏱11:30am-9:15pm; 🛜 🍴 🌿) 🌱 This airy, plant-adorned restaurant, known locally as P&E's, sits on the top floor of Thornes Marketplace and is the town's premier natural-foods restaurant. It serves delectable vegetarian and seafood dishes, often with an Asian bend.

Bela — VEGETARIAN $$
(☏413-586-8011; www.belaveg.com; 68 Masonic St; mains $9-13; ⏱noon-8:30pm Tue-Sat; 🍴 🌿) 🌱 This cozy vegetarian restaurant puts such an emphasis on fresh ingredients that the chalkboard menu changes daily depending on what local farmers are harvesting. Cash only.

Drinking & Entertainment

For a smallish town, Northampton sees a great line-up of indie bands, folk artists and jazz musicians, who play at the restored **Calvin Theatre** (☏413-586-8686; www.iheg.com; 19 King St) or other smaller venues around town.

Public Garden (p61), Boston

Northampton Brewery BREWPUB
(www.northamptonbrewery.com; 11 Brewster Ct;
⊙11:30am-1am; 🛜 🅿️) 🍴 The oldest operating
brewpub in New England enjoys a loyal summertime following thanks to its generously
sized outdoor deck and delicious libations.

Diva's LESBIAN
(www.divasofnoho.com; 492 Pleasant St; ⊙10pm-
2am Tue-Sat) The city's main gay-centric club
hosts dance nights, drag shows, Latin nights
and other high-energy weekly events. Located
about a mile south of the main intersection
on Rte 5.

Deerfield

While the modern commercial center is in
South Deerfield, it's Historic Deerfield 6
miles to the north that history buffs swarm
to, where zoning and preservation keep the
rural village looking like a time warp to the
18th century – sleepy, slow and without
much to do other than look at the period
buildings.

The main (OK, the only) street of Historic
Deerfield is simply called the Street, and it
runs parallel to US 5/MA 10. Follow the signs
from I-91.

⊙ Sights & Activities

Historic Deerfield Village HISTORIC BUILDINGS
(☑413-774-5581; www.historic-deerfield.org; the
Street; adult/child $14/5; ⊙9:30am-4:30pm Apr-
Dec) The main street of Historic Deerfield
Village escaped the ravages of time and now
presents a noble prospect: a dozen houses
dating from the 1700s and 1800s, well pre-
served and filled with period furnishings
that reflect their original occupants. It costs
nothing to stroll along the Street and admire
the buildings from outside.

Quinnetukut II Riverboat Cruise BOAT TOUR
(⊙Jul–mid-Oct; 👪) For a junket on the Connecticut River, catch a riverboat cruise on
the *Quinnetukut II*. A lecturer fills you in on
the history, geology and ecology of the river
during the 12-mile, 1½-hour ride, and you'll
pass under the elegant French King Bridge.
Cruises are run from July to mid-October
by the **Northfield Mountain Recreation
& Environmental Center** (☑800-859-2960;
www.gdfsuezna.com/riverboat-cruise; MA 63;
adult/child $12/6; ⊙cruises 11am, 1:15pm & 3pm
Fri-Sun). To get to the departure point, take
I-91 north to exit 27, then MA 2 east, then
MA 63 north. Call ahead for reservations.

🛏 Sleeping & Eating

Deerfield Inn INN $$$
(☑413-774-5587; www.deerfieldinn.com; the Street;
r incl breakfast $220-315; ❄🛜🅰️) This estab-
lishment, smack in the heart of the historic
district, has 24 modernized, spacious rooms.
The inn, built in 1884, was destroyed by fire
and rebuilt in 1981. During the tourist sea-
son, the inn's tavern serves lunch fare.

ℹ Information

In town, across from the Deerfield Inn, **Hall Tavern
Visitor Center** (☑413-775-7133; www.historic
-deerfield.org; the Street; ⊙9:30am-4:30pm
Apr-Dec) has maps, brochures and ticket sales.

Shelburne Falls

This artisan community's main drag (Bridge
St) is tiny and charming, only three blocks
long but with a passel of interesting gal-
leries and craft shops. Forming the back-
ground are mountains, the Deerfield River
and a pair of picturesque bridges that cross
it – one made of iron, the other covered in
flowers.

Shelburne Falls is just off MA 2 on MA 116.

⊙ Sights & Activities

Bridge of Flowers BRIDGE
FREE Shelburne Falls lays on the hype a bit
thick, yet one can't deny that its bridge of
flowers makes for a photogenic civic center-
piece. Volunteers have been maintaining it
since 1929. Over 500 varieties of flowers,
shrubs and vines flaunt their colors on the
400ft-long span from early spring through
to late fall. Access to the bridge is from
Water St.

Glacial Potholes RIVER
(Deerfield Ave) **FREE** Stones trapped swirling
in the roiling Deerfield River have been
grinding into the rock bed at this loca-
tion ever since the ice age. The result: 50
near-perfect circles in the riverbed, includ-
ing the largest known glacial pothole (39ft
diameter) in the world.

A hydroelectric dam overlooking this site
now controls the flow of the river over the
potholes, so it's possible that on your visit
the water will be completely obscuring the
holes. Either way it's worth a look – if the
flow is a trickle, you readily see the circles;
if it's raging, you'll feel like you're at Niagara
Falls. The potholes are at the end of Deer-
field Ave.

Deerfield Valley Canopy Tours
ADVENTURE SPORTS

(☏ 800-532-7483; www.deerfieldzipline.com; 7 Main St/MA 2, Charlemont; zip $91; ⊘ 10am-5pm Apr-Nov) Ready to fly? This zip line lets you unleash your inner Tarzan on a treetop glide above the Deerfield River Valley. The three-hour outing includes three rappels and 11 zips that get progressively longer. The hardest part is stepping off the first platform – the rest is pure exhilaration!

Children are welcome to join in the fun as long as they are at least 10 years old and weigh a minimum of 70lb. Charlemont is 7 miles west of Shelburne Falls.

Zoar Outdoor
RAFTING

(☏ 800-532-7483; www.zoaroutdoor.com; 7 Main St/MA 2, Charlemont; tours from $40; ⊘ 9am-5pm; ♿) This outfitter offers all sorts of splashy fun from white-water rafting to canoeing and kayaking the Deerfield River. No experience? No problem. Zoar's enthusiastic guides adeptly provide newbies with all the ABCs. It's a family-friendly scene with several activities geared especially for kids.

🛏 Sleeping

Dancing Bear Guest House
GUESTHOUSE $$

(☏ 413-625-9281; www.dancingbearguesthouse. com; 22 Mechanic St; r incl breakfast $139; ❄ 🛜) Everything the town has to offer is within easy walking distance of this c 1825 guesthouse. The owners are welcoming, the breakfast home-cooked and the rooms squeaky clean. It's like staying with old friends – a perfect choice for travelers who want a truly local experience.

✕ Eating

West End Pub
PUB $$

(☏ 413-625-6216; www.westendpubinfo.com; 16 State St; mains $11-24; ⊘ 11am-9pm Tue-Sun) Shelburne Falls' favorite place for a drink also serves an expanded menu of tasty pub fare. Best of all, it has a fantastic deck jutting out above the Deerfield River and directly overlooking the Bridge of Flowers.

Gypsy Apple Bistro
FUSION $$$

(☏ 413-625-6345; 65 Bridge St; mains $20-40; ⊘ 5-9pm Thu-Sun) When a place starts you off with warm bread and olive-caper tapenade you know it's gonna be good. The menu showcases French-inspired fare with a New England twist, such as rainbow trout in sherry butter or gnocchi with local mushrooms. Seating is limited, so call ahead for reservations.

🍷 Drinking

Mocha Maya's
CAFE

(☏ 413-625-6292; www.mochamayas.com; 47 Bridge St; ⊘ 7am-5pm, later some Fri & Sat; 🛜) ✎ No matter what your thirst, Mocha Maya's is the place, pouring everything from organic fair-trade coffee to blackberry martinis. Occasional live music and poetry readings as well.

ℹ Information

Shelburne Falls Visitor Center (☏ 413-625-2526; www.shelburnefalls.com; 75 Bridge St; ⊘ 10am-4pm Mon-Sat, noon-3pm Sun May-Oct) Helps with accommodations in the area.

Amherst

This college town, a short drive from Northampton, is built around the mega **University of Massachusetts** (UMass; www. umass.edu) and two small colleges, the liberal **Hampshire College** (www.hampshire.edu) and the prestigious **Amherst College** (www.am herst.edu). Contact the admissions offices for campus tours and event information.

🛏 Sleeping & Eating

Amherst Inn
B&B $$

(☏ 413-253-5000; www.allenhouse.com; 257 Main St; d incl breakfast $105-195; ❄) A stately, blue, three-story Victorian with Tudor detailing, this haunted-looking B&B sits in the midst of some old shade trees with fine garden landscaping. The friendly Swedish innkeepers also operate the Allen House Inn, just out of town.

Amherst Coffee
CAFE $

(☏ 413-256-8987; www.facebook.com/Amherst Coffee; 28 Amity St; snacks $6-12; ⊘ 6:30am-12:30am Mon-Sat, 8am-11pm Sun) Coffee shop by day, wine and whiskey bar by night, this place is surprisingly urbane for little Amherst. The limited menu features a selection of charcuterie, cheese and other Italian-style snacks. Stop in for a drink before or after catching a flick at the on-site Amherst Cinema.

Antonio's Pizza by the Slice
PIZZERIA $

(www.antoniospizza.com; 31 N Pleasant St; slices $2-3; ⊘ 10am-2am; ♿) Amherst's most popular pizza features a vast variety of toppings, flavorings and spices.

The Berkshires

Tranquil towns and a wealth of cultural attractions are nestled in these cool green hills. For more than a century the Berkshires have been a favored retreat for wealthy Bostonians and New Yorkers. And we're not just talking Rockefellers – the entire Boston symphony summers here as well. The **Berkshire Visitors Bureau** (🕿 413-743-4500; www.berkshires.org; 66 Allen St, Pittsfield; ⊙10am-5pm) provides information on the whole region.

Lee

Welcome to the towniest town in the Berkshires. A main street, both cute and gritty, runs through the center, curving to cross some railroad tracks. On it you'll find a hardware store, a bar and a few places to eat including a proper diner favored by politicians desiring photo ops with working-class folks. Most travelers pass through Lee simply because it's near a convenient exit off the Mass Pike. The main draw is the prestigious **Jacob's Pillow Dance Festival** (🕿413-243-0745; www.jacobspillow.org; 358 George Carter Rd, Becket; ⊙mid-Jun–Aug) on the outskirts of town.

Lee, just off exit 2 of I-90, is the gateway to Lenox, Stockbridge and Great Barrington. US 20 is Lee's main street, and leads right into Lenox, about a 15-minute drive away.

Bridge of Flowers (p72), Shelburne Falls
PHIL HABER PHOTOGRAPHY/GETTY IMAGES ©

◉ Sights

October Mountain State Forest   FOREST
(www.mass.gov/dcr; 317 Woodland Rd; ⊙dawn-dusk) Most out-of-towners who venture to the Berkshires head to the Mt Greylock State Reservation to see the state's highest peak, leaving October Mountain State Forest, a 16,127-acre state park and the largest tract of green space in Massachusetts, to the locals.

Hidden amid the hardwoods, Buckley Dunton Reservoir – a small body of water stocked with bass – is a great spot for canoeing. For hikers, a 9-mile stretch of the **Appalachian Trail** pierces the heart of the forest through copses of hemlock, spruce, birch, and oak. To get there from Lee, follow US 20 west for 3 miles and look for signs.

🛏 Sleeping

Motels in Lee are clustered around I-90 exit 2, on heavily trafficked US 20.

For a list of area accommodations, visit www.leelodging.org.

October Mountain State
Forest   CAMPGROUND $
(🕿877-422-6762; www.mass.gov/dcr; 317 Woodland Rd; tent sites $12-17) This state forest campground, near the shores of the Housatonic River, has 47 sites with hot showers. To find the campground, turn east off US 20 onto Center St and follow the signs.

Jonathan Foote 1778 House   B&B $$
(🕿413-243-4545; www.1778house.com; 1 East St; r incl breakfast $150-245; 🕸🛜) An old Georgian farmhouse set in spacious grounds with shady maple trees and stone walls. Stay here for antiquated fireplaces, appropriately decorated rooms and hearty breakfasts.

🍴 Eating

While Joe's Diner is the main draw, you'll also find a Chinese joint, a good bakery and a health food store in the center of town.

Joe's Diner   DINER $
(🕿413-243-9756; 85 Center St; mains $4-9; ⊙5:30am-8:00pm Mon-Fri, 5:30am-3:30pm Sat, 7am-1pm Sun) There's no better slice of blue-collar Americana in the Berkshires than Joe's Diner, at the north end of Main St. Norman Rockwell's famous painting of a policeman sitting at a counter talking to a young boy, *The Runaway* (1958), was inspired by this diner. Take a look at the repro of it above the counter.

Joe's has barely changed a wink, and not just the stools – think typical bacon-and-eggs diner fare.

ℹ Information

Lee Chamber of Commerce (☎413-243-0852; www.leechamber.org; 3 Park Pl; ☉10am-4pm Mon-Sat) Maintains an information booth on the town green in summer.

Lenox

The refined village of Lenox is the cultural heart of the Berkshires, thanks to the open-air **Tanglewood Music Festival** (☎888-266-1200; www.tanglewood.org; 297 West St/MA 183, Lenox; ☉late Jun-early Sep). One of the country's premier music series, Tanglewood hosts the Boston Symphony Orchestra and guest artists like James Taylor and Yo-Yo Ma.

🛏 Sleeping

Cornell in Lenox   B&B $$
(☎413-637-4800; www.cornellbb.com; 203 Main St; r incl breakfast from $149; @🛜) With three historic houses on 4 acres, Cornell offers a variety of comfortable room layouts and friendly, accommodating service.

Birchwood Inn   INN $$$
(☎413-637-2600; www.birchwood-inn.com; 7 Hubbard St; r incl breakfast $249-379; ❄🛜❄) The oldest house in Lenox (1767), the Birchwood Inn offers gorgeous period rooms, scrumptious breakfasts and warm hospitality.

🍴 Eating

Haven Cafe & Bakery   CAFE $
(☎413-637-8948; www.havencafebakery.com; 8 Franklin St; mains $8-15; ☉7:30am-3pm; 🛜🍴) It looks like a cafe, but the sophisticated food evokes a more upscale experience. Try inventive egg dishes for breakfast or fancy salads and sandwiches for lunch – all highlighting local organic ingredients.

★ Nudel   AMERICAN $$$
(☎413-551-7183; www.nudelrestaurant.com; 37 Church St; mains $22-26; ☉5:30-9:30pm Tue-Sun) A driving force in the area's sustainable-food movement, just about everything on Nudel's menu is seasonally inspired and locally sourced. Incredible flavors. Nudel doesn't take reservations, so arrive early to avoid a long wait.

OFF THE BEATEN TRACK

HANCOCK SHAKER VILLAGE

Just west of the town of Pittsfield, **Hancock Shaker Village** (www.hancockshakervillage.org; US 20; adult/youth/child $20/8/free; ☉10am-5pm mid-Apr–Oct; 🚻) is a fascinating museum illustrating the lives of the Shakers, the religious sect that founded the village in 1783. The Shakers believed in communal ownership, the sanctity of work and celibacy, the latter of which led to their demise. Their handiwork – graceful in its simplicity – includes wooden furnishings and 20 buildings, the most famous of which is the round stone barn.

Williamstown

Cradled by the Berkshire's rolling hills, Williamstown is a picture-perfect New England college town revolving around the leafy campus of **Williams College** (www.williams.edu). It's a mini cultural capital, with two stellar art museums holding down opposite ends of the town. In summer months, the **Williamstown Theatre Festival** (☎413-597-3400; www.wtfestival.org; 🚻) mounts a mix of contemporary works by up-and-coming playwrights, and classics attracting plenty of well-known thespians to the stage.

◉ Sights

★ Clark Art Institute   MUSEUM
(www.clarkart.edu; 225 South St; adult/child $20/free; ☉10am-5pm Tue-Sun) Set on a gorgeous 140-acre campus, the Sterling & Francine Clark Art Institute is a gem among small art museums. The collections are particularly strong in the impressionists, but the highlight is the rich collection of paintings by Winslow Homer, George Inness and John Singer Sargent.

Williams College Museum of Art   MUSEUM
(www.wcma.org; 15 Lawrence Hall Dr; ☉10am-5pm, closed Wed Sep-May) **FREE** Gracing the center of town, this is the sister museum of the Clark Art Institute. Around half of its 13,000 pieces comprise the American Collection, with substantial works by notables such as Edward Hopper *(Morning in a City)*, Winslow Homer and Grant Wood, to name a few.

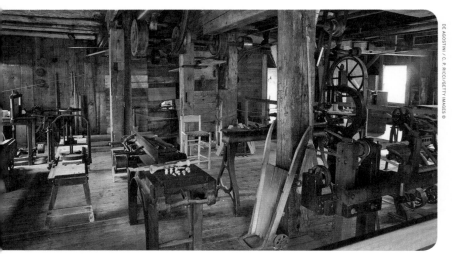

Hancock Shaker Village (p75)

🛏 Sleeping

River Bend Farm B&B   B&B **$$**
(☑ 413-458-3121; www.riverbendfarmbb.com; 643 Simonds Rd/US 7; r incl breakfast $120; ☉ Apr-Oct; ❄🐾) Step back to the 18th century in this Georgian Colonial B&B, furnished with real-deal antiques and boasting five fireplaces. Four doubles share two bathrooms. Located one mile north of town. Credit cards are not accepted.

Maple Terrace Motel   MOTEL **$$**
(☑ 413-458-9677; www.mapleterrace.com; 555 Main St; d incl breakfast $128-188; 🐾❄) The Maple Terrace is a simple yet cozy 15-room place on the eastern outskirts of town. The Swedish innkeepers have snazzed up the grounds with gardens that make you want to linger.

Field Farm   INN **$$$**
(☑ 413-458-3135; www.thetrustees.org/field-farm; 554 Sloan Rd; r incl breakfast $195-325; @🐾❄) This one-of-a-kind inn offers an artful blend of mid-20th-century modernity and timeless mountain scenery. Six clean-lined rooms are spacious and fitted with handcrafted furnishings that reflect the modernist Bauhaus style of the house. The grounds feature miles of lightly trodden walking trails.

🍴 Eating & Drinking

Pappa Charlie's Deli   DELI **$**
(☑ 413-458-5969; 28 Spring St; mains $5-9; ☉ 7:30am-8pm) The stars themselves created the lunch sandwiches that bear their names. (Order a Politician and get anything you want on it.)

★ Mezze Bistro & Bar   FUSION **$$**
(☑ 413-458-0123; www.mezzerestaurant.com; 777 Cold Spring Rd/US 7; mains $16-28; ☉ 5-9pm) Situated on 3 acres, Mezze takes a farm-to-table approach, beginning with an edible garden right on site. Much of the rest of the seasonal menu, from small-batch micro-brews to organic meats, is locally sourced as well.

Hops & Vines   BEER GARDEN
(www.hopsandvinesma.com; 16 Water St; ☉ noon-10pm Tue-Sat, to 8pm Sun; 🐾) This two-sided bar and restaurant offers an experience for every mood. The quirky, casual ambience and excellent beer selection make 'Hops' the hands-down favorite, but some occasions call for a classy dining room like 'Vines'.

North Adams

Gritty North Adams is a former manufacturing center that was long dominated by the vast campus of the Sprague Electric Company. When Sprague closed in the 1980s, the site was converted into the USA's largest contemporary museum. North Adams is also a jumping-off point for Mt Greylock, the highest mountain in Massachusetts.

◉ Sights

MASS MoCA   MUSEUM
(www.massmoca.org; 87 Marshall St; adult/child $18/8; ⊙10am-6pm Jul & Aug, 11am-5pm Wed-Mon Sep-Jun; 🚪) The museum encompasses 222,000 sq ft and over 25 buildings, including art construction areas, performance centers and 19 galleries. One gallery is the size of a football field, giving installation artists the opportunity to take things into a whole new dimension. Bring your walking shoes!

Mt Greylock State Reservation   PARK
See p22.

🛏 Sleeping & Eating

Porches   BOUTIQUE HOTEL $$
(☑413-664-0400; www.porches.com; 231 River St; r incl breakfast $135-225; ❋🖥🎙📶) Across the street from MASS MoCA, the artsy rooms here offer soothing color palettes, tasteful furnishings and – appropriately – private porches.

Public Eat & Drink   PUB FOOD $$
(☑413-664-4444; www.publiceatanddrink.com; 34 Holden St; mains $10-22; ⊙4-10pm Mon-Wed, 11:30am-10pm Thu-Sun; ✏) Come to this cozy North Adams pub for an excellent selection of craft beers and gourmet pub fare, such as brie burgers, flatbread pizzas and bistro steak.

Stockbridge

This timeless New England town, with not even a single traffic light, looks like something straight out of a Norman Rockwell painting. No coincidence! Rockwell (1894–1978), the most popular illustrator in US history, lived on Main St and used the town and its residents as subjects. See his slice-of-life artwork up close, as well has his studio, at the evocative **Norman Rockwell Museum** (☑413-298-4100; www.nrm.org; 9 Glendale Rd/MA 183; adult/child $18/6; ⊙10am-5pm).

Tyringham

POP 330
The village of Tyringham, between Lee and Monterey, is the perfect destination for an excursion into the heart of the countryside. Once the home of a Shaker community (1792–1874), Tyringham is now famous for its **Gingerbread House**, an architectural fantasy designed at the beginning of the

20th century by sculptor Henry Hudson Kitson, whose best-known work – a statue of Captain Parker as a minuteman – graces the Lexington Green. Kitson's fairy-tale thatched-roofed cottage is at 75 Main St on the north side of the village; it's readily visible from the road, though the interior is not open to the general public.

After leaving Tyringham bear west at the fork in the road toward Monterey and continue your journey snaking over gentle hills and past farmland along the scenic back road into Great Barrington. En route you'll discover some **woodsy places** to hike, a roadside **pond** that begs a dip and a couple of **art studios**.

Great Barrington

Woolworths, diners and hardware stores have given way to art galleries, urbane boutiques and locavore restaurants on Main St, Great Barrington. The picturesque Housatonic River flows through the center of town, with the **River Walk** (www.gbriverwalk.org) offering a perfect perch from which to admire it. Access the walking path from Main St (behind Rite-Aid) or from Bridge St. At the intersection of Main and Railroad Sts, you'll find an artful mix of galleries and eateries.

Gypsy Joynt   CAFE $$
(☑413-644-8811; www.gypsyjoyntcafe.net; 293 Main St; mains $10-15; ⊙11am-midnight Wed-Sat, to 9pm Sun, to 4pm Mon; 📶✏) This is a family affair, with three generations pitching in to serve innovative pizzas, beefy sandwiches and bountiful salads. Most everything is organic and locally sourced. The Gypsy Joynt also throws in great coffee, live music and a super boho atmosphere.

Baba Louie's   PIZZA $$
(☑413-528-8100; www.babalouiespizza.com; 286 Main St; pizzas $12-18; ⊙11:30am-9:30pm; 📶✏) Baba's is known for its wood-fired pizza with organic sourdough crust, and guys with dreadlocks. There's a pizza for every taste, including vegan and gluten-free options.

Barrington Brewery   BREWPUB
(www.barringtonbrewery.net; 420 Stockbridge Rd; mains $8-20; ⊙11:30am-9:30pm; 📶) ✐ Solar-powered microbrews – you know you're in Great Barrington! Outdoor seating is divine on a balmy summer night. Located 2 miles north of the town center on the road to Stockbridge.

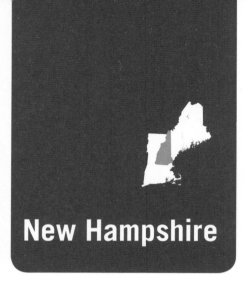

New Hampshire

This state has the scale of things just right for residents and travelers: the towns are small and personable, the mountains majestic and rugged and the fall foliage scenery is spectacular.

The heart of New Hampshire is unquestionably the granite peaks of the White Mountain National Forest (WMNF). Outdoor enthusiasts of all stripes flock to New England's highest range (6288ft at Mt Washington) for cold-weather skiing, summer hiking and brilliant fall foliage scenery. And don't be fooled by that politically conservative label that people stick on the state. The state mantra, 'Live Free or Die,' indeed rings from every automobile license plate, but residents here pride themselves on their independent spirit more than right-wing politics.

History

Named in 1629 after the English county of Hampshire, New Hampshire was one of the first American colonies to declare its independence from England in 1776. During the 19th-century industrialization boom, the state's leading city, Manchester, became such a powerhouse that its textile mills were the world's largest.

New Hampshire played a high-profile role in 1944 when president Franklin D Roosevelt gathered leaders from 44 Allied nations to remote Bretton Woods for a conference discussing how to rebuild global capitalism. It was at the Bretton Woods Conference that the World Bank and the International Monetary Fund emerged.

In 1963 New Hampshire, long famed for its anti-tax sentiments, found another way to raise revenue – by becoming the first state in the USA to have a legal lottery.

❶ Information

Welcome centers are situated at major state border crossings.

New Hampshire Division of Parks & Recreation (☑ 603-271-3556; www.nhstateparks.org) Offers information on hiking, biking, camping and other outdoor activities.

New Hampshire Division of Travel & Tourism Development (☑ 603-271-2665; www.visitnh. gov) Order a visitor's guide and check out the adventure itineraries.

White Mountains

What the Rockies are to Colorado the White Mountains are to New Hampshire. New England's loftiest mountain range is a magnet for adventurers, with boundless opportunities for everything from hiking and kayaking to skiing. Those who prefer to take it in from the comfort of a car seat won't be disappointed either, as scenic drives wind over rugged mountains rippling with waterfalls, sheer rock faces and sharply cut gorges.

You'll find information on the White Mountains at ranger stations throughout the White Mountain National Forest (www.fs.usda.gov/ whitemountain) and at chambers of commerce in the towns along the way.

Mount Washington Valley

Stretching north from the eastern terminus of the Kancamagus Hwy, Mt Washington Valley includes the towns of Conway, North Conway and Bartlett. Every conceivable outdoor activity is available. The area's hub and biggest town, North Conway, is also a center for outlet shopping, including some earthy stores such as LL Bean.

Sights & Activities

★ **Conway Scenic Railroad**   TRAIN
(☑603-356-5251; www.conwayscenic.com; 38 Norcross Circle, North Conway; ☺mid-Jun–Oct; ♿) The **Notch Train** (adult/child 4-12yr/child 1-3yr from $55/39/11), built in 1874 and restored in 1974, offers New England's most scenic journey. The spectacular five- to 5½-hour trip passes through Crawford Notch. Accompanying live commentary recounts the railroad's history and folklore. Reservations required.The same company operates the antique steam **Valley Train** (adult/child 4-12yr/child 1-3yr from $16.50/11.50/free), which makes a shorter journey south through the Mt Washington Valley, stopping in Conway and Bartlett. Look for seasonal excursions such as the Pumpkin Patch Express in October and the Polar Bear Express in November and December.

★ **Mount Washington Observatory Weather Discovery Center**   MUSEUM
(☑603-356-2137; www.mountwashington.org; 2779 White Mountain Hwy, North Conway; adult/child 7-17yr $2/1; ☺10am-5pm) If you don't have time to drive to the summit of Mt Washington but you think wild weather is cool, take an hour to explore this small but fascinating weather museum instead. Shoot an air cannon, interrupt a minitornado and learn why temperatures are so extremely cold atop Mt Washington. What happens when you push the red button inside the mock observatory shack? All we'll say is, hold on tight.

Echo Lake State Park   PARK
(www.nhstateparks.org; River Rd; adult/child 6-11yr $4/2) Two miles west of North Conway via River Rd, this placid mountain lake lies at the foot of **White Horse Ledge**, a sheer rock wall. A scenic trail circles the lake, which has a small beach. There is also a mile-long auto road and hiking trail leading to the 700ft-high **Cathedral Ledge**, with panoramic White Mountains views. Both Cathedral Ledge and White Horse Ledge are excellent

for rock climbing. This is also a fine spot for swimming and picknicing.

Sleeping

North Conway in particular is thick with sleeping options from cozy inns to resort hotels.

White Mountains Hostel   HOSTEL $
(☑603-447-1001; www.whitemountainshostel.com; 36 Washington St, Conway; dm $20, r $20-30; ☎) ✐ Set in an early-1900s farmhouse, this cheery and environmentally conscientious hostel has dorm bedrooms with bunk beds, five private rooms, and a communal lounge and kitchen. Excellent hiking, bicycling and kayaking opportunities are all found nearby. Our only gripe is the location, which is 5 miles south of the action in North Conway.

Not a party hostel, but a great choice if you want to explore the outdoors.

Cranmore Inn   B&B $$
(☑603-356-5502; www.cranmoreinn.com; 80 Kearsarge St; r incl breakfast $149-369; ☎✷) Under

White Mountains & Mt Washington Valley

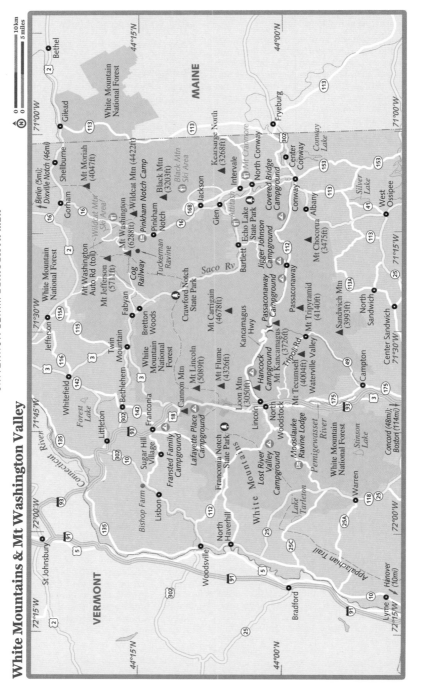

new ownership and recently renovated, the Cranmore has lost the country frills. Rooms now sport a fresh, more contemporary style. In addition to standard rooms, there are several two-room suites and one apartment with a kitchen. The inn has been operating as a country inn since 1863. There's a year-round hot tub on-site, perfect for posthike sore muscles.

Hampton Inn North Conway   HOTEL **$$$**
(☎ 603-356-7736; www.hamptoninn3.hilton.com; 1788 White Mountain Hwy; r from $279; ✳ @ 🛜 ✉) Traveling with high-energy kids? Let them loose in the 5000-sq-ft indoor water park, with two slides, at this super welcoming location of the national chain.

Eating

Peach's   CAFE **$**
(☎ 603-356-5860; www.peachesnorthconway.com; 2506 White Mountain Hwy; breakfast $6-10, lunch $8-9; ⏱ 7am-2:30pm) Away from the in-town bustle, this perennially popular little house is an excellent option for soups, sandwiches and breakfast. Who can resist fruit-smothered waffles and pancakes, and fresh-brewed coffee, served in somebody's cozy living room?

Moat Mountain Smoke House & Brewing Co   PUB FOOD **$$**
(☎ 603-356-6381; www.moatmountain.com; 3378 White Mountain Hwy; mains $10-23; ⏱ 11:30am-midnight) With its great food, on-point service and tasty homemade beers, Moat Mountain wins best all around for New Hampshire brewpubs. Come here for a wide array of American fare, with a nod to the South: BBQ sandwiches, beefy chili, juicy burgers, wood-grilled pizzas, and a delicious curried crab and corn bisque. Wash it down with one of the numerous brews made on-site.

ℹ Information

Mt Washington Valley Chamber of Commerce
(☎ 603-356-5701; www.mtwashingtonvalley.org; 2617 White Mountain Hwy; ⏱ 9am-5pm) Tourist information just south of North Conway's town center. Hours are notoriously unreliable.

Kancamagus Highway

The winding Kancamagus Hwy (NH 112) between Lincoln and Conway runs right through the WMNF and over Kancamagus Pass (2868ft). Unspoiled by commercial development, the paved road offers easy access to US Forestry Service (USFS) campgrounds, hiking trails and fantastic scenery.

Though the Kancamagus Hwy was paved only in 1964, its name dates to the 17th century. The route is named for Chief Kancamagus (The Fearless One). In about 1684 Kancamagus assumed the powers of *sagamon* (leader) of the Penacook Native American tribe. He was the final *sagamon*, succeeding his grandfather, the great Passaconaway, and his uncle Wonalancet. Kancamagus tried to maintain peace between the indigenous peoples and European explorers and settlers, but the newcomers pushed his patience past breaking point. He finally resorted to battle to rid the region of Europeans, but in 1691 he and his followers were forced to escape northward.

The Kancamagus Hwy (NH 112) runs for 35 miles from Lincoln to Conway. Since there are no services along the highway, the towns are convenient for picking up picnic supplies before hitting the trails.

🏃 Activities

The WMNF is laced with excellent hiking trails of varying difficulty. For detailed trail-by-trail information, stop at any of the WMNF ranger stations or the White Mountains Attractions Association.

Lincoln Woods Trail   HIKING
The trailhead for this 2.9-mile, 1157ft-elevation trail is on the Kancamagus Hwy, 5 miles east of I-93. Among the easiest and most popular in the forest, the trail ends at the Pemigewasset Wilderness Boundary (elevation 1450ft).

Wilderness Trail   HIKING
The easy Wilderness Trail begins where the Lincoln Woods Trail ends, at Pemigewasset Wilderness Boundary, and it continues for 6 miles to Stillwater Junction (elevation 2060ft). From there you can follow the Cedar Brook and Hancock Notch Trails to return to the Kancamagus Hwy at a point on the road that is some miles east of the Lincoln Woods trailhead parking lot.

🛏 Sleeping

Village of Loon Mountain   RESORT **$$**
(☎ 800-228-2968, 603-745-3401; www.villageofloon.com; Kancamagus Scenic Byway, Lincoln; ste $119-244, apt $105-269; 🛜 ✉) This lodge has basic, modern suites that sleep at least four people, as well as condos right on the mountainside, so you can ski straight to the chairlift. Recreational facilities are unlimited here, with several pools and hot tubs, tennis courts, horseback riding, hiking and biking on offer.

Econo Lodge at Loon   MOTEL **$$**
(☑ 603-745-3661, 800-762-7275; www.
econolodgeloon.com; US 3, Loon Mountain; r incl
breakfast $85-130; 🛜 ☒) This large, nicely
outfitted lodge caters to skiers and snow-
mobilers, who appreciate the sauna, hot
tub and spa. Fifty-three rooms – many with
kitchenettes – offer decent value.

❶ Information

**Conway Village Chamber of Commerce Info
Booth** (☑ 603-447-2639; 250 Main St/NH 16,
Conway; ⊘ 9am-5pm Apr-Oct) The eastern
gateway to the scenic highway.

White Mountains Attractions Association
(☑ 603-745-8720; www.visitwhitemountains.
com; 200 Kancamagus Hwy; ⊘ 8:30am-5pm
Apr-Oct) You can pick up detailed hiking
brochures for area trails here. It's about a mile
west of Conway.

North Woodstock & Lincoln

The twin towns of Lincoln and North Wood-
stock break up the drive between the Kan-
camagus Hwy and Franconia Notch State
Park, so they are a handy place to stop for a
bite or a bed. The towns straddle the Pem-
igewasset River at the intersection of NH
112 and US 3. Ratchet up the adrenaline
by zipping 2000ft down a hillside while
strapped to just a cable with the treetop zip

line at **Alpine Adventure** (☑ 603-745-9911;
www.alpinezipline.com; 41 Main St, Lincoln; zips
from $64; ⊘ 11am-4pm).

🛏 Sleeping & Eating

Woodstock Inn   INN **$$**
(☑ 603-745-3951; www.woodstockinnnh.com; US 3;
r incl breakfast with shared/private bath from
$147/178; ✳️🛜) Anchoring downtown North
Woodstock, this Victorian country inn features 34 individually appointed rooms
across five separate buildings (three in a
cluster, two across the street), each with
modern amenities but old-fashioned style.
For dinner, you have your choice of the on-
site upscale restaurant and microbrewery
(Woodstock Station & Microbrewery).

**Woodstock Inn Station
& Brewery**   PUB **$$**
(☑ 603-745-3951; www.woodstockinnnh.com; US 3;
mains $12-24; ⊘ 11:30am-10pm) On warm days
the sunny front patio is a nice place to eat,
drink and watch the world go by. Former-
ly a railroad station, this eatery tries to be
everything to everyone, with more than
150 items on the menu. Pasta, sandwiches
and burgers are the most interesting. The
beer-sodden rear tavern is one of the most
happening places in this neck of the woods.

SCENIC DRIVE: WHITE MOUNTAIN NATIONAL FOREST

One of New England's finest, the 35-mile **Kancamagus Hwy** (NH 112) is a beauty of a
road cutting through the **White Mountain National Forest** between Conway and Lin-
coln. Laced with excellent hiking trails, scenic lookouts and swimmable streams, this is
as natural as it gets. There's absolutely no development along the entire highway, which
reaches its highest point at **Kancamagus Pass** (2868ft).

Pick up brochures and hiking maps at the **Saco Ranger District Office** (☑ 603-
447-5448; 33 Kancamagus Hwy; ⊘ 8am-4:30pm) at the eastern end of the highway near
Conway. On the western end, stop by the National Forest desk at the **White Mountains
Visitor Center** (p78) in North Woodstock.

Coming from Conway, 6.5 miles west of the Saco ranger station, you'll see **Lower
Falls** on the north side of the road – stop here for the view and a swim. No trip along this
highway is complete without taking the 20-minute hike to the breathtaking cascade of
Sabbaday Falls; the trail begins at Mile 15 on the south side of the road. The best place
to spot moose is along the shores of **Lily Pond**; stop at the roadside overview at Mile 18.
At the Lincoln Woods ranger station, which is near the Mile 29 marker, cross the suspen-
sion footbridge over the river and hike 3 miles to **Franconia Falls**, the finest swimming
hole in the entire national forest, complete with a natural rock slide. Parking anywhere
along the highway costs $3 per day (honor system) or $5 per week; just fill out an enve-
lope at any of the parking areas.

The White Mountain National Forest is ideal for campers, and you'll find several camp-
grounds run by the forest service accessible from the Kancamagus Hwy. Most are on a
first-come, first-served basis; pick up a list at the Saco ranger station.

White Mountain National Forest (p78)

ℹ Information

Lincoln/Woodstock Chamber of Commerce
(☏ 603-745-6621; www.lincolnwoodstock.com; 126 Main St/NH 112, Lincoln; ☺ 9am-5pm Mon-Fri) Offers area information.

White Mountains Visitor Center (☏ 603-745-8720, National Forest 603-745-3816; www.visit whitemountains.com; 200 Kancamagus Hwy; ☺ visitor info 8:30am-5pm, National Forest desk 9am-3pm daily mid-May–Oct, Fri, Sat & Sun only Nov–mid-May) A life-size stuffed moose (not real) sets a scene for adventure while brochures and trail maps provide the details. You can also buy a White Mountain National Forest Pass here ($3/5 per day/week), which is required for extended stops at national forest trailheads.

Franconia Notch State Park

Franconia Notch is the most celebrated mountain pass in New England, a narrow gorge shaped over the eons by a rushing stream slicing through the craggy granite. I-93, in places feeling more like a country road than a highway, runs straight through the state park. The **Franconia Notch State Park visitor center** (☏ 603-745-8391; www.nhstateparks.org; I-93, exit 34A; ☺ 9am-5pm mid-May–Oct), 4 miles north of North Woodstock, can give you details on hikes in the park, which range from short nature walks to day-long treks.

Take a walk or a bike ride on the 8.8-mile **bike path** that tracks the Pemigewasset River and links Flume Gorge and Cannon Mountain. Bike rentals are available at the tramway (half/full day $25/40).

◉ Sights & Activities

Cannon Mountain Aerial Tramway   CABLE CAR
(☏ 603-823-8800; www.cannonmt.com; I-93, exit 34B; round-trip adult/child 6-12yr $17/14; ☺ 9am-5pm late May–mid-Oct; ♿) This tramway shoots up the side of Cannon Mountain, offering a breathtaking view of Franconia Notch. In 1938 the first passenger aerial tramway in North America was installed on this slope. It was replaced in 1980 by the current, larger cable car, capable of carrying 80 passengers up to the summit in five minutes – a 2022ft, 1-mile ride. Or, visitors can hike up the mountain and take the tramway down.

Flume Gorge   HIKING
(www.nhstateparks.org; adult/child 6-12yr $16/13; ☺ 9am-5pm May-Oct) To see this natural wonder, take the 2-mile self-guided nature walk that includes the 800ft boardwalk through the Flume, a natural cleft (12ft to 20ft wide) in the granite bedrock. The granite walls tower 70ft to 90ft above you, with moss and other plants growing from precarious niches and crevices. Signs explain how nature formed this natural phenomenon. A nearby covered bridge is thought to be one of the oldest in the state, perhaps erected as early as the 1820s.

Echo Lake   BEACH
(☏ 603-823-8800; I-93, exit 34C; adult/child 6-11yr $4/2; ☺ 10am-5pm mid-Jun–Aug) Despite its proximity to the highway, this little lake at the foot of Cannon Mountain is a pleasant

place to pass an afternoon swimming, kayaking or canoeing (rentals $20 per hour) in crystal-clear waters. And many people do. The small beach gets packed, especially on weekends.

Franconia Town & Around

A few miles north of the notch via I-93, Franconia is a tranquil town with splendid mountain views and a poetic attraction: Robert Frost's farm. As a rule, the further the distance from the highway, the more picturesque and pristine the destination. Accordingly, the little towns of **Bethlehem** (north along NH 142), **Littleton** (north along NH 18), and the tiny village of **Sugar Hill** (a few miles west along tranquil NH 117) are delightful. All are perfect for whiling away an afternoon driving down country roads, poking into antique shops, browsing farm stands and chatting up the locals at divey diners.

⊙ Sights & Activities

★ **Frost Place**   HISTORIC SITE
(☑ 603-823-5510; www.frostplace.org; 158 Ridge Rd, Franconia; adult/child $5/3; ☺1-5pm Thu-Sun Jun, 1-5pm Wed-Mon Jul–mid-Sep, 10am-5pm mid-Sep–mid-Oct) Robert Frost (1874–1963) is America's most renowned and best-loved poet of the mid-20th century. For several years he lived with his wife and children on a farm near Franconia, now known as the Frost Place. Many of his best and most famous poems describe life on this farm and the scenery surrounding it, including 'The Road Not Taken' and 'Stopping by Woods on a Snowy Evening,' and the years spent here were some of the most productive and inspired of his life. The farmhouse has been kept as faithful to the period as possible, with numerous exhibits of Frost memorabilia.

In the forest behind the house there is a half-mile nature trail. Frost's poems are mounted on plaques in sites appropriate to the things the poems describe, and in several places the plaques have been erected at the exact spots where Frost was inspired to compose the poems. To find Frost's farm, follow NH 116 south from Franconia. After exactly a mile, turn right onto Bickford Hill Rd, then left onto unpaved Ridge Rd. It's a short distance along on the right.

Sugar Hill Sampler   MUSEUM
(☑ 603-823-8478; www.sugarhillsampler.com; Sunset Hill Rd, Sugar Hill Village; ☺9:30am-5pm Sat &

Sun mid-Apr–mid-May, 9:30am-5pm mid-May–Oct, 10am-4pm Nov-Dec, closed Jan–mid-Apr) **FREE** It all started with a collection of heirlooms amassed by the Aldrich family over the many years they have lived in Sugar Hill Village. These days, this collection has expanded to include all sorts of local memorabilia dating from 1780, housed in an old barn built by the Aldrich ancestors themselves. There's also a store selling homemade arts and crafts and edibles.

Franconia Sports Shop   BICYCLE RENTAL
(☑ 603-823-5241; www.franconiasports.com; 334 Main St, Franconia; road/mountain bikes per day $20/28) Offers bike rental.

🛏 Sleeping

Pinestead Farm Lodge   LODGE $
(☑ 603-823-8121; www.pinesteadfarmlodge.com; 2059 Easton Rd/NH 116, Franconia; r/apt from $65/150) This is a rarity in Franconia: a working farm. The family here rents clean, simple rooms in several apartments with shared bath and communal kitchen/sitting rooms. You can also rent entire apartments. Hosts Bob and Kathleen Sherburn, whose family has owned the property since 1899, have an assortment of cattle, chickens, ducks and horses. If you come in March or April, you can watch maple sugaring.

★ **Sugar Hill Inn**   INN $$
(☑ 800-548-4748, 603-823-5621; www.sugarhillinn.com; NH 117, Sugar Hill Village; r/ste incl breakfast from $145/215; 🛜) This restored 1789 farmhouse sits atop a hill that has stunning panoramic views, especially in the fall, when the sugar maples lining the hill are ablaze. Sixteen acres of lawns and gardens and 14 romantic guest rooms (many with gas fireplaces and Jacuzzis), not to mention the delectable country breakfast, make this a top choice.

Kinsman Lodge   B&B $$
(☑ 603-823-5686; www.kinsmanlodge.com; 2165 Easton Rd/NH 116, Franconia; s/d with shared bath incl breakfast from $65/105; 🛜) This lodge built in the 1860s has nine comfortable, unpretentious rooms on the 2nd floor. The 1st floor consists of cozy common areas and an inviting porch. The homemade breakfasts, with offerings such as buttermilk pancakes and luscious omelets, are superb.

Horse & Hound Inn   INN $$
(☑ 800-450-550, 603-823-5501; www.horseandhoundnh.com; 205 Wells Rd, Franconia; r/ste incl

NEW HAMPSHIRE LEAF-PEEPS

In fall the White Mountains turn vibrant shades of crimson and gold, capped by rocky peaks. Already awesome when the trees are green, the vistas are unparalleled when the leaves turn. The classic foliage driving tour is the Kancamagus Hwy (p81), a gorgeous mountain road between Lincoln and Conway.

➡ The western end of the highway boasts **Franconia Notch** (p83), where you can marvel at the colors on numerous trails.

➡ Ride the tramway up **Cannon Mountain** (p83) for lofty views of the great rainbow of colors and fantastic photo opportunities.

➡ **Crawford Notch** (p86) offers hikes for more hardy types, including one up to Mt Washington.

breakfast from $130/275; ☎) This pleasant country inn offers eight frilly rooms set in a cozy 1830 farmhouse. Some rooms feature antiques, while others – those with rosy curtains and floral bedspread – can be a bit over the top, but it's good value for the area. The property also has a restaurant, the Hunt Room, which serves American fare in a cozy setting (mains $8 to $35).

Bishop Farm B&B **$$**
(☏ 603-838-2474; www.bishopfarm.com; 33 Bishop Cutoff, Lisbon; r/ste incl breakfast from $160/199, cottages from $149; ☎) This family-run farmhouse has seven attractively designed rooms done in a trim, contemporary look (but with old-fashioned touches such as claw-foot tubs) and six cottages with full kitchens. The house is set on 19 forested acres, which means snowshoeing and cross-country skiing in the winter and mountain biking or hiking at other times. The front porch is an idyllic spot for enjoying the scenery. It's 9 miles west of Franconia, just off US 302.

Franconia Inn INN **$$**
(☏ 800-473-5299, 603-823-5542; www.franconia inn.com; NH 116, Franconia; r/ste incl breakfast from $135/180; ☺closed Apr–mid-May; ☎☒) This excellent 29-room inn, just 2 miles south of Franconia, is set on a broad, fertile, pine-fringed river valley. You'll find plenty of common space and well-maintained guest rooms.

Inn at Sunset Hill B&B **$$**
(☏ 603-823-7244; www.sunsethillhouse.com; 231 Sunset Hill Rd, Sugar Hill Village; r incl breakfast from $110; ☎) This 'Grand Inn,' as it is called, lives up to its moniker. All 30 rooms, spread across two buildings, have lovely views of either the mountains or the golf course next door. The pricier rooms have hot tubs, fireplaces and private decks, but all the rooms

are lovely. The dining room is a formal affair, but there is also a more casual tavern.

✕ Eating

Many of Franconia's inns offer fine dining, including the Horse & Hound, Sugar Hill Inn, Franconia Inn and Sunset Hill House.

Polly's Pancake Parlor AMERICAN **$$**
(☏ 603-823-5575; www.pollyspancakeparlor.com; NH 117, Sugar Hill Village; mains $10-18; ☺7am-3pm) Attached to a 19th-century farmhouse 2 miles west of Franconia, this local institution offers pancakes, pancakes and more pancakes. They're excellent, made with home-ground flour and topped with the farm's own maple syrup, eggs and sausages. Polly's cob-smoked bacon is divine, and sandwiches (made with homemade bread) and quiches are also available.

★ **Cold Mountain Cafe** INTERNATIONAL **$$**
(☏ 603-869-2500; www.coldmountaincafe.com; 2015 Main St, Bethlehem; sandwiches $8-13, mains $13-22; ☺11am-3pm & 5.30-9pm Mon-Sat, 10am-2pm Sun) Hands down the best restaurant in the region, this casual cafe and gallery has an eclectic, changing menu, featuring gourmet sandwiches and salads at lunch and rich bouillabaisse, seafood curry and rack of lamb at dinner. Everything is prepared with the utmost care and nicely presented, but the atmosphere is very relaxed. Be prepared to wait for your table (outside, since the place is cozy). There's regular live music, from jazz to folk.

Coffee Pot DINER **$**
(☏ 603-444-5722; www.thecoffeepotrestaurant. com; 30 Main St, Littleton; mains up to $10; ☺6:30am-4pm Mon-Fri, to 2pm Sat, to noon Sun) Sit at the counter and you'll be gabbing with the locals before you even order your eggs. A friendly spot for getting the Littleton lowdown.

Cannon Mountain Aerial Tramway (p83)
PREMIUM UIG/GETTY IMAGES ©

Chang Thai
THAI **$$**

(☑603-444-8810; www.changthaicafe.com; 77 Main St, Littleton; mains $13-20; ⊙11:30am-9pm Mon-Fri, 12-9pm Sat & Sun) Listen to live jazz as you savor pad thai, green curry and other well seasoned dishes. Check online for jazz nights.

☆ Entertainment

Colonial Theater
THEATER, CINEMA

(☑603-869-3422; www.bethlehemcolonial.org; Main St, Bethlehem; live shows from $18) This classic theater in downtown Bethlehem is a historic place to hear the jazz, blues and folk musicians that pass through this little town. The venue also serves as a cinema, showing independent and foreign films.

🔲 Shopping

Harman's Cheese & Country Store
FOOD

(☑603-823-8000; www.harmanscheese.com; 1400 NH 117, Sugar Hill Village; ⊙ 9:30am-5pm daily May-Oct, to 4:30 Mon-Sat Nov-Apr) If you need to pack a picnic for your hike – or if you simply wish to stock up on New England goodies before heading home – don't miss this country store, which stocks delicious cheddar cheese (aged for at least two years), maple syrup, apple cider (in season) and addictive spicy dill pickles.

ℹ️ Information

Bethlehem Chamber of Commerce (☑888-845-1957; www.bethlehemwhitemtns.com; 2182 Main St/NH 302, Bethlehem; ⊙10am-4pm Jun-Oct, hours vary Nov-Feb, rest of year by appt)

Franconia Notch Chamber of Commerce (☑ 603-823-5661; www.franconianotch.org; 121 Main St, Franconia; ⊙9am-5pm; 🛜) Southeast of the town center.

Bretton Woods & Crawford Notch

Before 1944 Bretton Woods was known primarily as a low-key retreat for wealthy visitors who patronized the majestic Mt Washington Hotel. After president Franklin D Roosevelt chose the hotel for the historic conference that established a new post-WWII economic order, the town's name took on worldwide recognition. The countryside, with Mt Washington looming above it, is as magnificent today as it was back then. The **Twin Mountain-Bretton Woods Chamber of Commerce** (☑800-245-8946; www.twinmountain.org; cnr US 302 & US 3; ⊙9am-5pm Jul & Aug, 9am-5pm Fri-Sun foliage season, closed rest of yr) information booth has details about the area.

The state's largest ski area, **Bretton Woods** (☑603-278-3320; www.brettonwoods. com; US 302; Sat, Sun & holidays lift ticket adult/child 13-17/child 6-12 & seniors $85/65/49, Mon-Fri $75/58/43) offers downhill and cross-country skiing, and a zip-line in warmer months (May to September).

US 302 heads south from Bretton Woods to Crawford Notch (1773ft) through stunning mountain scenery ripe with towering cascades. **Crawford Notch State Park** (☑ 603-374-2272; www.nhstateparks.org; 1464 US Route 302; adult/child 6-11yr $4/2) maintains an extensive system of hiking trails, including short hikes around a pond and to a waterfall, and a longer trek up Mt Washington.

🛏️ Sleeping

AMC Highland Center
LODGE **$$**

(☑information 603-278-4453, reservations 603-466-2727; www.outdoors.org/lodging/whitemountains/highland; NH 302, Bretton Woods; dm incl breakfast & dinner adult/child $106/55, s/d incl breakfast & dinner $153/89) This cozy Appalachian Mountain Club (AMC) lodge is set amid the splendor of Crawford Notch, an ideal base for hiking the many trails crisscrossing the Presidential Range. The grounds are beautiful, rooms are basic but comfortable, meals are hearty and guests are outdoor enthusiasts. Discounts are available for AMC members. The information center, open to the public, has loads of information about regional hiking.

★ **Omni Mt Washington Hotel & Resort**   HOTEL $$$
(☑ 603-278-1000; www.omnihotels.com; 310 Mt Washington Hotel Rd, Bretton Woods; r from $339, ste $869; ✳@🖥⛷) Open since 1902 this grand hotel maintains a sense of fun – note the moose's head overlooking the lobby and the framed images of local wildflowers in many of the guest rooms. It also offers 27 holes of golf, red-clay tennis courts, an equestrian center and a spa. A sunset cocktail on the back porch, with the mountains before you, is perfection. There's a $27.25 daily resort fee.

Mount Washington

From Pinkham Notch (2032ft), on NH 16 about 11 miles north of North Conway, a system of hiking trails provides access to the natural beauties of the Presidential Range, including lofty Mt Washington (6288ft), the highest mountain east of the Mississippi and north of the Smoky Mountains.

Hikers need to be prepared: Mt Washington's weather is notoriously severe and can turn on a dime. Dress warmly – not only does the mountain register New England's coldest temperatures (in summer, the average at the summit is 45°F/7°C) but unrelenting winds make it feel colder than the thermometer reading. In fact, Mt Washington holds the record for the USA's strongest wind gust – 231mph!

The **Pinkham Notch Visitor Center** (☑ 603-278-4453; www.outdoors.org; NH 16; ☺6:30am-10pm May-Oct, to 9pm Nov-Apr), run by the AMC, is the area's informational nexus for like-minded adventurers and a good place to buy hiking necessities, including topographic trail maps and the handy *AMC White Mountain Guide*.

One of the most popular trails up Mt Washington begins at the visitor center and runs 4.2 strenuous miles to the summit, taking four to five hours to reach the top and a bit less on the way down.

If your quads aren't up for a workout, the **Mt Washington Auto Road** (☑ 603-466-3988; www.mountwashingtonautoroad.com; 1 Mt Washington Auto Rd, off NH 16; car & driver $28, extra adult/child 5-12yr $8/6; ☺7:30-6pm early Jun-Aug, shorter hours mid-May–early Jun & Sep-mid-Oct), 2.5 miles north of Pinkham Notch

Camp, offers easier summit access, weather permitting.

While purists walk, and the out-of-shape drive, the quaintest way to reach the summit is to take the **Mt Washington Cog Railway** (☑ 603-278-5404; www.thecog.com; 3168 Bass Station Rd; adult/child 4-12yr $68/39; ☺May-Oct). Since 1869 coal-fired steam-powered locomotives have followed a 3.5-mile track up a steep mountainside trestle for a jaw-dropping excursion.

Dolly Copp Campground (☑ 603-466-2713, reservations 877-444-6777; www.fs.usda.gov; NH 16; tent & RV sites $22; ☺mid-May–mid-Oct) is a USFS campground 6 miles north of the AMC's Pinkham Notch facilities.

Hanover & Around

The archetypal New England college town, Hanover has a town green that is bordered on all four sides by the handsome brick edifices of Dartmouth College. Virtually the whole town is given over to this Ivy League school; chartered in 1769, Dartmouth is the nation's ninth-oldest college.

Main St, rolling down from the green, is surrounded by perky pubs, shops and cafes that cater to the collegian crowd. The Appalachian Trail runs along Main St right through downtown.

◉ Sights

Dartmouth College   COLLEGE
(☑ 603-646-1110; www.dartmouth.edu) Hanover is all about Dartmouth College, so hit the campus. Join a free student-guided **campus walking tour** (☑ 603-646-2875; https://admis

---

LOCAL KNOWLEDGE

NEW HAMPSHIRE'S WINE & CHEESE TRAIL

Watch out, Vermont. New Hampshire's small cheese producers are multiplying, and small wineries are popping up left and right. The tourism board put together an excellent leaflet, *New Hampshire Wine, Chocolate & Cheese Trails*, detailing three itineraries across 21 farms and wineries, including a few cider producers. Pick it up from any tourist office or download it from the web at www.agriculture.nh.gov/publications-forms/agricultural-development.htm

sions.dartmouth.edu; 6016 McNutt Hall), or grab a map at the admissions office across from the green in McNutt Hall. Maps are also available online. Don't miss the **Baker-Berry Library**, splashed with the grand *Epic of American Civilization,* painted by the outspoken Mexican muralist José Clemente Orozco (1883–1949), who taught at Dartmouth in the 1930s.

Hood Museum of Art MUSEUM
(☑603-646-2808; http://hoodmuseum.dartmouth.edu; E Wheelock St; ⊙10am-5pm Tue & Thu-Sat, to 9pm Wed, noon-5pm Sun) **FREE** Shortly after the university's founding in 1769 Dartmouth began to acquire artifacts of artistic or historical interest. Since then the collection has expanded to include nearly 65,000 items, which are housed at the Hood Museum of Art. The collection is particularly strong in American pieces, including Native American art. One of the highlights is a set of Assyrian reliefs from the Palace of Ashurnasirpal that date to the 9th century BC. Special exhibits often feature contemporary artists.

🛏 Sleeping & Eating

Hanover Inn INN $$$
(☑603-643-4300, 800-443-7024; www.hanoverinn.com; 2 E Wheelock St, cnr W Wheelock & S Main

Sts; r from $249; @🖥📶🐾) A 2800lb handmade granite table now anchors the lobby at the recently revamped Hanover Inn, the city's loveliest guesthouse. Owned by Dartmouth College, the inn has nicely appointed rooms with custom artwork, collegiate-style throws, and elegant wood furnishings. It has a farm-to-table restaurant on site. Pets are $50 per night.

Lou's DINER $
(☑603-643-3321; www.lousrestaurant.net; 30 S Main St; breakfast $8-12, lunch $9-12; ⊙6am-3pm Mon-Fri, 7am-3pm Sat & Sun) A Dartmouth institution since 1947, this is Hanover's oldest establishment, always packed with students meeting for a coffee or perusing their books. From retro tables or the Formica-topped counter, order typical diner food like eggs, sandwiches and burgers. The bakery items – I'm talking about you, ginger molasses cookie – are also highly recommended.

Canoe Club Bistro CAFE $$
(☑603-643-9660; www.canoeclub.us; 27 S Main St; lunch $12-24, dinner $10-23; ⊙11:30am-11:30pm) 🎵 This smart cafe does a fine job with grilled food – not just burgers and steaks, but also a range of farm-to-table fare with global accents including a crispy pork schnitzel and Malay curry shrimp. There's also live entertainment nightly, anything from acoustic to jazz to a Monday night magic show.

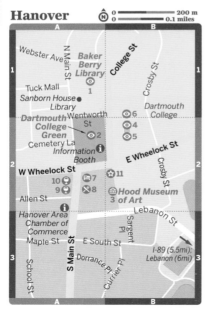

Hanover
⊙ 0 ─────── 200 m
0 ─────── 0.1 miles

SCENIC DRIVE: MONADNOCK VILLAGES

The region surrounding Mt Monadnock is a web of narrow winding roads connecting classic New England towns, and one could easily spend a few days exploring this picturesque countryside.

➝ **Fitzwilliam**, south of the mountain on NH 119, has a town green surrounded by lovely old houses and a graceful town hall with a steeple rising to the heavens.

➝ **Harrisville**, northwest of Peterborough via NH 101, is a former mill village that looks much as it did in the late 1700s, when the textile industry in these parts was flourishing. Today its mill buildings have been converted into functionally aesthetic commercial spaces.

➝ **Hancock**, north of Peterborough on NH 123, is another quintessential New England village. The town's showpiece is one of the oldest continuously operating inns in New England: **Hancock Inn** (☑800-525-1789, 603-525-3318; www.hancockinn.com; 33 Main St; r incl breakfast $180-300; ☎), has 15 rooms, each with its own unique charms. Dome ceilings (in rooms that used to be part of a ballroom), fireplaces and private patios are some of the features. The cozy dining room is open for breakfast and dinner.

➝ **Hillsborough Center**, 14 miles north of Hancock on NH 123, is another classic, not to be confused with Hillsborough Lower Village and Upper Village. Steeped in the late 18th and early 19th centuries, the trim little town has a number of art studios.

➝ **Walpole**, northwest of Keene along NH 12, is another gem. Locals descend from surrounding villages to dine at **Burdick Chocolate** (p40).

Drinking & Entertainment

Murphy's on the Green PUB

(☑603-643-4075; wwwmurphysonthegreen.com; 11 S Main St; mains $12-24; ☺4pm-12:30am Mon-Thu, 11am-12:30am Fri-Sun) This classic collegiate tavern is where students and faculty meet over pints (it carries over 10 beers on tap, including local microbrews like Long Trail Ale) and satisfying pub fare (mains $12 to $24). Stained-glass windows, church-pew seating and book-lined shelves enhance the cozy atmosphere.

Hopkins Center
for the Arts PERFORMING ARTS

(☑603-646-2422; www.hop.dartmouth.edu; 4 E Wheelock St) A long way from the big-city lights of New York and Boston, Dartmouth hosts its own entertainment at this outstanding performing-arts venue. The season brings everything from movies to live performances by international companies.

❶ Information

Hanover Area Chamber of Commerce

(☑603-643-3115; www.hanoverchamber.org; 53 S Main St, Suite 208; ☺9am-4pm Mon-Fri) For tourist information. It's inside the Nugget Building.

Monadnock State Park & Around

The climb to the 3165ft summit of **Mt Monadnock** (www.nhstateparks.org; 116 Poole Rd, NH 124, Jaffrey; adult/child 6-11yr $4/2) is rocky and steep, but the view from the boulder-capped summit is oh-so-worth-the-burn. Mt Monadnock, in the southwestern corner of the state, is the most hiked summit in New England. Monadnock, 'Mountain That Stands Alone' in Algonquian, is relatively isolated from other peaks, which means hikers who make the 5-mile round-trip to the summit are rewarded with unspoiled views of three states. Best bet for first-timers? Hike up on the White Dot Trail and return via the White Cross Trail.

The best posthike reward? Everyone knows it's a heaping scoop of ice cream from **Kimball Farm** (www.kimballfarm.com; 158 Turnpike Rd; small scoops $5; ☺ice cream 10am-10pm) just up the road. Choose from more than 50 flavors, including chocolate raspberry, maple walnut, and coffee Oreo. For a drink or an overnight stay near the mountain, try the quirky charms of the **Monadnock Inn** (☑603-532-7800; www.monadnockinn.com; 379 Main St; r $110-190), where the tavern is cozy and your room may include a wire birdcage.

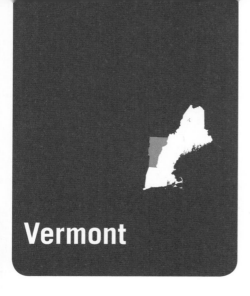

Vermont

Green, upbeat and a little bit quirky, Vermont is a pretty place that embraces its natural beauty with a respectful joie de vivre.

Vermont, we like your crunchy soul. For anyone who appreciates slow-paced meandering and nonstop scenic beauty, Vermont is Paradise. And the eating is darn good too, from the artisanal cheeses to Ben & Jerry's ice cream to the buckets of maple syrup. Fortunately, there are plenty of ways to work it off: hike the trails of the Green Mountains, paddle a kayak on Lake Champlain or hit the snowy slopes.

Vermont gives true meaning to the word rural. Its capital would barely rate as a small town in other states and even its largest city, Burlington, has just 42,200 contented souls. The countryside is a blanket of rolling green, with 80% of the state forested and most of the rest given over to some of the prettiest farms you'll ever see. The Green Mountain State is also home to more than 100 covered bridges. So take your time, meander down quiet side roads, stop in those picturesque villages, and sample a taste of the good life.

VERMONT FACTS

Nickname Green Mountain State

Population 626,500

Area 9217 sq miles

Capital city Montpelier (population 7755)

Other city Burlington (population 42,200)

Sales tax 6%

Birthplace of Mormon leader Brigham Young (1801–77), President Calvin Coolidge (1872–1933)

Home of More than 100 covered bridges

Politics Independent streak, leaning Democrat

Famous for Ben & Jerry's ice cream

Sudsiest state Most microbreweries per capita in the USA

Driving distances Burlington to Brattleboro 151 miles; Burlington to Boston 216 miles

History

Frenchman Samuel de Champlain explored Vermont in 1609, becoming the first European to visit these lands long inhabited by the native Abenaki.

Vermont played a key role in the American Revolution in 1775 when Ethan Allen led a local militia, the Green Mountain Boys, to Fort Ticonderoga, capturing it from the British. In 1777 Vermont declared independence as the Vermont Republic, adopting the first New World constitution to abolish slavery and establish a public school system. In 1791 Vermont was admitted to the USA as the 14th state.

The state's independent streak is as long and deep as a vein of Vermont marble. Long a land of dairy farmers, Vermont is still largely agricultural and has the lowest population of any New England state.

❶ Information

Vermont Dept of Tourism (www.vermontvaca tion.com) Online information by region, season and other user-friendly categories.

Vermont Public Radio (VPR; www.vpr.net) Vermont's excellent statewide public radio station. The radio frequency varies across the state, but the following selection covers most areas: Burlington (northwestern Vermont – 107.9); Brattle-

boro (southeastern Vermont – 88.9); Manchester (southwestern Vermont – 106.9); and St Johnsbury (northeastern Vermont – 88.5).

Vermont State Parks (☑ 888-409-7579; www. vtstateparks.com) Complete camping and parks information.

Northern Vermont

Boasting some of New England's lushest and prettiest landscapes, northern Vermont cradles the fetching state capital of Montpelier, the ski mecca of Stowe, the vibrant college town of Burlington and the state's highest mountains.

Vermont & New Hampshire

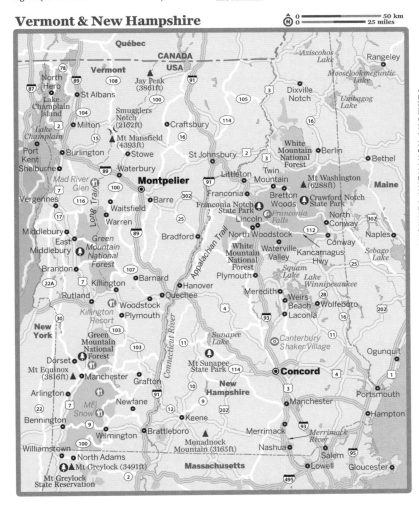

VERMONT LEAF-PEEPS

Here are a few spots to see Vermont's famous fall foliage at its best:

Mt Mansfield Vermont's highest peak is gorgeous when draped in fall colors, especially when an early snowfall dusts the summit white. The best panoramic perspectives are from Stowe, Jeffersonville, Cambridge and Underhill. Hikers can also experience the full sweep of color from the mountaintop; one of the prettiest routes is the Sunset Ridge Trail in Underhill State Park.

Grafton (p108) Villages don't get any cuter than Grafton, which looks like it was airlifted in from an earlier century. The white clapboard buildings are photogenic when contrasted against fiery leaves and a brilliant blue sky.

Lake Willoughby (p100) The technicolor majesty of changing maples looks especially dramatic on the steep slopes surrounding this fjordlike lake in the Northeast Kingdom.

Killington K1 Gondola (p102) The same lift that whisks skiers and mountain bikers to the mountaintop in winter and summer also affords spectacular panoramic views for fall leaf peepers.

Vermont Rte 100 A road-tripper's dream, this classic driving route through the heart of the Green Mountains shows off Vermont's farm country in its full autumnal splendor.

Merck Forest (✆802-394-7836; www.merckforest.org; 3270 VT 315; ⊙9am-4pm; 🖐) ✔ Climb to the barn meadow at this environmental education center in southwestern Vermont for breathtaking vistas of the Taconic Mountains in bright rainbow colors.

Montpelier

America's smallest capital, Montpelier is a thoroughly likable town of period buildings backed by verdant hills and crowned by the gold-domed 19th-century **State House** (www.vtstatehouse.org; 115 State St; ⊙tours 10am-3:30pm Mon-Fri, 11am-2:30pm Sat Jul-Oct) FREE. Tours of the capitol building run on the hour and the half hour. Right across the street, the **Capitol Region Visitors Center** (✆802-828-5981; 134 State St; ⊙6am-5pm Mon-Fri, 9am-5pm Sat & Sun) has tourist information.

Bookstores, boutiques and restaurants throng the town's twin thoroughfares, State and Main Sts. Forget about junk food – Montpelier prides itself on being the only state capital in the USA without a McDonald's! The bakery-cafe **La Brioche** (www.neci.edu/labrioche; 89 Main St; pastries $1-5, sandwiches $5-8; ⊙7am-6pm Mon-Fri, to 3pm Sat), run by students from Montpelier's New England Culinary Institute, gets an A-plus for its innovative sandwiches and flaky French pastries.

Stowe & Around

With Vermont's highest peak, **Mt Mansfield** (4393ft), as its backdrop, Stowe ranks as Vermont's classiest ski destination. It packs all the alpine thrills you could ask for – both cross-country and downhill skiing, with gentle runs for novices and challenging drops for pros. Cycling, hiking and kayaking take center stage in other seasons. Lodgings and eateries are thick along VT 108 (Mountain Rd), which continues northwest from Stowe village to the ski resorts.

◉ Sights & Activities

In warm weather, don't miss the drive through dramatic **Smugglers Notch**, northwest of Stowe on VT 108 (closed by heavy snows in winter). This narrow pass slices through mountains with 1000ft cliffs on either side. Roadside trails lead into the surrounding high country.

★ **Ben & Jerry's**
Ice Cream Factory FACTORY
(✆802-882-1240; www.benjerrys.com; 1281 VT 100, Waterbury; adult/child under 13yr $4/free; ⊙9am-9pm Jul–mid-Aug, to 7pm mid-Aug–Oct, 10am-6pm Nov-Jun; 🖐) A far cry from the abandoned Burlington gas station where ice cream pioneers Ben Cohen and Jerry Greenfield first set up shop in 1978, this legendary factory, just north of I-89 in Waterbury, draws crowds for tours that include a campy moo-vie and a taste tease of the latest flavor.

Behind the factory, a mock cemetery holds 'graves' of Holy Cannoli and other long-forgotten flavors.

Long Trail

HIKING

Vermont's 300-mile Long Trail, which passes west of Stowe, follows the crest of the Green Mountains and runs the entire length of Vermont, with rustic cabins, lean-tos and campsites along the way. Its caretaker, the **Green Mountain Club** (☑ 802-244-7037; www. greenmountainclub.org; 4711 Waterbury-Stowe Rd/VT 100) , has full details on the Long Trail and shorter day hikes around Stowe.

★ Stowe Recreation Path

OUTDOORS

(www.stowerec.org/paths; 🚹 📷) This flat-to-gently rolling 5.3-mile path offers a fabulous four-season escape for all ages, as it rambles through woods, meadows and outdoor sculpture gardens along the west branch of the Little River, with sweeping views of Mt Mansfield in the distance. Bike, walk, skate or ski, and perhaps take a dip in one of the swimming holes along the way. If you're traveling with your dog, veer onto the 1.8-mile **Quiet Path** extension (p110), open only to joggers and walkers, and their dogs.

Umiak Outdoor Outfitters

OUTDOORS

(☑ 802-253-2317; www.umiak.com; 849 S Main St; ⊙ 9am-6pm) Rents kayaks, snowshoes and Telemark skis; offers boating lessons; and leads river and moonlight snowshoe tours.

AJ's Ski & Sports

EQUIPMENT RENTAL

(☑ 802-253-4593, 800-226-6257; www.stowesports. com; 350 Mountain Rd; ⊙ 9am-6pm) Rents bikes, and skiing and snowboarding equipment in the town center.

🛌 Sleeping

Stowe Motel & Snowdrift

MOTEL, APARTMENT $$

(☑ 802-253-7629, 800-829-7629; www.stowemo tel.com; 2043 Mountain Rd; r $108-188, ste $192-208, apt $172-240; @ 🕿 🛎) Active guests will do just fine at this motel: it's set on 16 acres and home to a tennis court, hot tubs, lawn games, and free bicycles or snowshoes for use on the adjacent Stowe Recreation Path. Units range from simple to deluxe.

Trapp Family Lodge

LODGE $$$

(☑ 802-253-8511, 800-826-7000; www.trappfamily. com; 700 Trapp Hill Rd; r from $295; @ 🕿 🛎 🛎) The setting is appropriately breathtaking, and you'd surely be forgiven if you broke into song. Surrounded by wide-open fields and mountain vistas, this Austrian-style chalet, built by Maria von Trapp of *Sound of Music* fame, boasts Stowe's best setting. Traditional lodge rooms are complemented by guesthouses scattered across the 2700-acre property. A network of trails offers stupendous hiking, snowshoeing and cross-country skiing. Pet fee is $50 per night.

🍴 Eating

Harvest Market

MARKET $

(☑ 802-253-3800; www.harvestatstowe.com; 1031 Mountain Rd; ⊙ 7am-5:30pm) Before heading for the hills, stop here for coffee, pastries, Vermont cheeses, sandwiches, gourmet deli items, wines and local microbrews.

VERMONT

KIM GRANT/GETTY IMAGES ©

Ben & Jerry's Ice Cream Factory

Stowe & Around

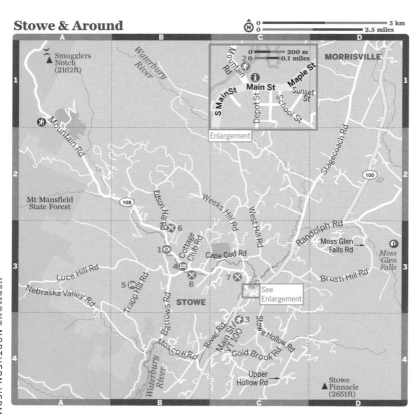

Stowe & Around

◎ Sights

✈ Activities, Courses & Tours

🛏 Sleeping

✕ Eating

Pie-casso   PIZZA **$$**
(☎802-253-4411; www.piecasso.com; 1899 Mountain Rd; sandwiches $9-13, pizza $11-22; ⊙11am-10pm Sun-Thu, to 11pm Fri & Sat) Organic arugula chicken salad and portobello panini supplement the menu of excellent hand-tossed pizzas. There's a bar and live music too.

Gracie's Restaurant   BURGERS **$$**
(☎802-253-8741; www.gracies.com; 18 Edson Hill Rd; mains $12-44; ⊙5pm until close) Halfway between the village and the mountain, this animated, dog-themed eatery serves big burgers, hand-cut steaks, Waldorf salad and garlic-laden shrimp scampi.

★Hen of the Wood   AMERICAN **$$$**
(☎802-244-7300; www.henofthewood.com; 92 Stowe St, Waterbury; mains $22-29; ⊙5-9pm Tue-Sat) ✿ Arguably the finest dining in northern Vermont, this chef-driven restaurant in Waterbury gets rave reviews for its innovative farm-to-table cuisine. The setting in a historic grist mill rivals the extraordinary food, which features densely flavored dishes, such as ham-wrapped rabbit loin and sheep's-milk gnocchi.

ℹ Information

Stowe Area Association (☎ 802-253-7321; www.gostowe.com; 51 Main St; ⊙ 9am-5pm Mon-Sat, to 8pm Jun-Oct & Jan-Mar) In the heart of the village.

Burlington

This hip college town on the shores of scenic Lake Champlain is one of those places that makes you think: wouldn't it be great to live here? The cafe and club scene is on par with a much bigger city, while the slow, friendly pace is pure small town. And where else can you walk to the end of Main St and paddle off in a kayak?

◎ Sights

Burlington's shops, cafes and pubs are concentrated around Church St Marketplace, a bustling brick-lined pedestrian mall midway between the University of Vermont and Lake Champlain.

★ **Shelburne Museum**   MUSEUM
(☎ 802-985-3346;   www.shelburnemuseum.org; 6300 Shelburne Rd/US 7, Shelburne; adult/youth 13-17yr/child 5-12yr $24/14/12; ⊙ 10am-5pm mid-May–Oct; 📱) Wear your walking shoes for this extraordinary 45-acre museum, which showcases a Smithsonian-caliber collection of Americana – 150,000 objects in all. The mix of folk art, decorative arts and more is housed in 39 historic buildings, most of

them relocated here from other parts of New England to ensure their preservation. Located 9 miles south of Burlington.

Shelburne Farms   FARM
See p30.

Magic Hat Brewery   BREWERY
(☎ 802-658-2739; www.magichat.net; 5 Bartlett Bay Rd, South Burlington; ⊙ 10am-7pm Mon-Sat Jun–mid-Oct, to 6pm Mon-Thu, to 7pm Fri & Sat mid-Oct-May, noon-5pm Sun year-round) Drink in the history of one of Vermont's most dynamic microbreweries on the fun, free, self-guided tour. Afterwards, sample a few of the eight brews on tap in the on-site Growler Bar. Recent samples included the Peppercorn Pilsner, made with pink peppercorns, and the Electric Peel, a grapefruit IPA.

🏃 Activities

Ready for outdoor adventures? Head to the waterfront, where options include boating on **Lake Champlain** and cycling, in-line skating and walking on the 7.5-mile shorefront **Burlington Bike Path**. Jump-off points and equipment rentals for all these activities are within a block of each other near the waterfront end of Main St.

Local Motion   BICYCLE RENTAL
(☎ 802-652-2453; www.localmotion.org; 1 Steele St; bicycles per day $32; ⊙ 9am-6pm Jul & Aug, 10am-6pm May & Jun, Sep & Oct; 📱) 🚲 Rents

VERMONT

BRIGITTE MERLE/GETTY IMAGES ©

Shelburne Museum

Burlington

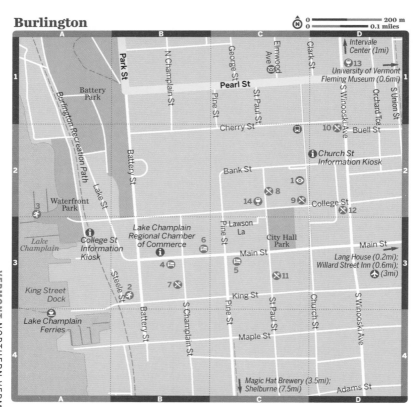

quality bikes beside the Burlington Bike Path between Main and King Sts.

Whistling Man Schooner Company SAILING
(☑802-598-6504; www.whistlingman.com; Boathouse, 1 College St; 2hr cruises adult/child under 12yr $50/35; ☺3 trips daily, late May–early Oct) Sail around Lake Champlain with the breeze in your hair and a Vermont microbrew in your hand on the 'Friend Ship,' a classic 43ft New England sloop. Captains are knowledgeable about the area, and passengers are welcome to bring food and drink on board. Private charters are also available. Reserve ahead.

🛏 Sleeping

Burlington's budget and midrange motels are on the outskirts of town, clustered along Shelburne Rd (US 7) in South Burlington, Williston Rd (US 2) east of I-89 exit 14, and US 7 north of Burlington in Colchester (I-89 exit 16).

Burlington Hostel HOSTEL $
(☑802-540-3043; www.theburlingtonhostel.com; 53 Main St; dm incl breakfast $40; ✱@☎) Just minutes from Church St and Lake Champlain, Burlington's hostel offers both mixed and single sex dorms, with eight beds per room.

Sunset House B&B B&B $$
(☑802-864-3790; www.sunsethousebb.com; 78 Main St; r $120-170; ☎) This sweet B&B features four tidy guest rooms. Bathrooms are shared, and there's a small common kitchen. This is the only B&B smack in the center of downtown.

Lang House B&B $$
(☑802-652-2500; www.langhouse.com; 360 Main St; r incl breakfast $199-259; ✱@☎) This may be Burlington's most elegant B&B, but you can still kick back and relax like the proletariat – this is Burlington, after all. This tastefully restored 19th-century Victorian home and carriage house occupies a centrally located spot not far from down-

Burlington

town. Reserve ahead for one of the 3rd-floor rooms with lake views.

Hilton Garden Inn
Burlington Downtown   HOTEL $$
(☏802-951-0099; www.hiltongardeninn3.hilton.com; 101 Main St; r from $229; P✳@�ⓢ☲) Hip *and* historic? Yep, and the combination works seamlessly at this Hilton Garden, which opened in 2015. Housed in a former armory, the hotel is within walking distance of Church St Marketplace and Lake Champlain. The airy pavilion lobby pops with bright colors and crisp decor. Rooms are a bit less exuberant but come with Serta beds, mini-fridges, and microwaves. Note that weekends book up far in advance. Parking is $16 per night and valet only.

★**Inn at Shelburne Farms**   INN $$$
(☏802-985-8498; www.shelburnefarms.org/stay dine; 1611 Harbor Rd, Shelburne; r with private/shared bath from $210/165, cottage from $320, guesthouse from $450; ☺May-Oct; ☎) At this historic 1400-acre estate (p30) on the shore of Lake Champlain, 7 miles south of Burlington, guests stay in a gracious, welcoming country manor house, or in one of four independent, kitchen-equipped cottages and guest houses scattered across the property. The attached farm-to-table restaurant is superb. And those lake sunsets? Ahhhh.

✗ Eating

On Saturday mornings, downtown City Hall Park hosts Burlington's thriving **farmers market** (www.burlingtonfarmersmarket.org).

August First Bakery & Cafe   BAKERY, PIZZERIA $
(☏802-540-0064; http://augustfirstvt.com; 149 South Champlain St; meals $9-14; ☺11:30am-5pm Mon-Thu, 11:30am-5pm & 6-9pm Fri, 8am-3pm Sat) Most days this bakery-cafe is a hot spot for a cup of coffee, sandwiches and its famous breads. Expect anything from traditional pepperoni to more exotic gorgonzola and pear pizzas and everything in between.

Penny Cluse Cafe   CAFE $
(☏802-651-8834; www.pennycluse.com; 169 Cherry St; mains $6-12.25; ☺6:45am-3pm Mon-Fri, 8am-3pm Sat & Sun) ✔ Did somebody say bucket-o-spuds? Oh yes, they did. And that's just the first thing listed on the enticing menu at Penny Cluse, one of Burlington's most popular downtown eateries. The kitchen also whips up pancakes, biscuits and gravy, omelets and tofu scrambles along with sandwiches, fish tacos, salads and excellent *chiles rellenos*. Expect long lines on weekends.

City Market   MARKET $
(☏802-861-9700; www.citymarket.coop; 82 S Winooski Ave; sandwiches $8-10; ☺7am-11pm) ✔ If there's a natural-foods heaven, it must look something like this downtown co-op: chock-full of local produce and products (with more than 1000 Vermont-based producers represented) and a huge takeout deli.

Stone Soup   VEGETARIAN $
(☏802-862-7616; www.stonesoupvt.com; 211 College St; buffet per lb $10.75, sandwiches under $10; ☺7am-9pm Mon-Fri, 9am-9pm Sat; ☎✔) Squeeze in at lunchtime for the small but excellent vegetarian- and vegan-friendly buffet

---

LOCAL KNOWLEDGE

A SECRET GARDEN

Hidden away less than 2 miles from Burlington's city center is one of Vermont's most idyllic green spaces. Tucked among the lazy curves of the Winooski River, the **Intervale Center** (www.intervale.org; 180 Intervale Rd) FREE encompasses a dozen organic farms and a delightful trail network, open to the public 365 days a year for hiking, biking, skiing, berry picking and more; check the website for details.

VERMONT NORTHERN VERMONT

at this longtime local favorite. Also good: homemade soups, sandwiches on home-baked bread, a salad bar and pastries.

★ **Pizzeria Verita**   PIZZA **$$**
(☑802-489-5644; www.pizzeriaverita.com; 156 Paul St; pizza $8-18; ⊘5-10pm Sun-Thu, to 11pm Fri & Sat) You can't walk two steps in Burlington without somebody recommending new-on-the-scene Pizzeria Verita. And their recom-mendation is spot-on. It's heaven on a thin crust. Step into this modernly rustic trat-toria (you know what we mean – wine casks for bar tables, etc) for the *quatro formaggi*, the *funghi rustico*, or the Ring of Fire with hot cherry peppers.

Blue Bird Tavern   INTERNATIONAL **$$**
(☑802-540-1786; http://bluebirdvermont.com; 86 Paul St; meals $9-25; ⊘ lunch & dinner) Burling-ton's most experimental locavore eatery fea-tures a seasonal menu with small and large plates – expect anything from hot oysters with seaweed aioli and maple sugar to mac 'n' cheese with peas, morel mushrooms and snails. Be sure to book.

Daily Planet   INTERNATIONAL **$$**
(☑802-862-9647; www.dailyplanet15.com; 15 Center St; mains $11-24; ⊘4-9pm Sun-Thu, to 9:30pm Fri & Sat; ☎☑) This stylish downtown haunt serves everything from confit duck poutine to burg-ers with tasty trimmings to pan-roasted lamb lollipops to caramelized sea scallops. The bar stays open until 2am nightly.

WORTH A TRIP

SCENIC DRIVE: VERMONT'S GREEN MOUNTAIN BYWAY

Following Vermont's Green Mountain spine through the state's rural heart, the **VT 100** rambles past rolling pastures speckled with cows, tiny villages with country stores and white-steepled churches, and verdant mountains criss-crossed with hiking trails and ski slopes. It's the quintessential side trip for those who want to slow down and experience Vermont's bucolic essence. The road runs south to north all the way from Massachusetts to Canada. Even if your time is limited, don't miss the scenic 45-mile stretch between Waterbury and Stockbridge, an easy detour off I-89. For details about attractions along the way, visit www.vermont-byways.us.

Leunig's Bistro   FRENCH **$$$**
(☑802-863-3759; www.leunigsbistro.com; 115 Church St; lunch $12-22, dinner $18-34; ⊘11am-10pm Mon-Thu, to 11pm Fri, 9am-11pm Sat, to 10pm Sun) With sidewalk seating and an elegant, tin-ceilinged dining room, this Parisian-style brasserie is a longstanding Burlington staple. It's as much fun for the people-watching (windows face busy Church St Marketplace) as for the excellent wine list and food.

🍸 Drinking & Nightlife

The free weekly *Seven Days* (www.7dvt.com) has event and entertainment listings.

Radio Bean   BAR
(www.radiobean.com; 8 N Winooski Ave; ⊘8am-2am Mon-Sat, 10am-2am Sun; ☎) This funky cafe-bar features its own low-power FM radio station, a trendy attached eatery serv-ing international street food, and live perfor-mances nightly which include jazz, acoustic music and poetry readings.

Vermont Pub & Brewery   MICROBREWERY
(www.vermontbrewery.com; 144 College St; mains $5-18; ⊘11:30am-1am Sun-Wed, to 2am Thu-Sat) Specialty and seasonal brews, including weekly limited releases, are made on the premises, and accompanied by British-style pub fare.

🛍 Shopping

You'll find boutiques and smart craft shops along Church St Marketplace. Don't miss the **Frog Hollow Craft Center** (www.froghol low.org; 85 Church St; ⊘10am-6pm Mon-Wed, to 8pm Thu-Sat, 11am-7pm Sun mid-Apr–Nov, reduced hours rest of the year) **FREE**, a collective featur-ing some of the finest work in Burlington.

❶ Information

University of Vermont Medical Center (☑802-847-0000; www.uvmhealth.org; 111 Colchester Ave; ⊘24hr) Vermont's largest hospital. Has a 24-hour level 1 trauma center.
Lake Champlain Regional Chamber of Com-merce (☑802-863-3489, 877-686-5253; www.vermont.org; 60 Main St; ⊘8am-5pm Mon-Fri) Downtown tourist office.

❶ Getting There & Away

Lake Champlain Ferries (☑802-864-9804; www.ferries.com; King St Dock; adult/child 6-12yr/car $8/3.10/30) runs ferries mid-June through September across the lake to Port Kent, NY (one hour 20 minutes).

LAKE CHAMPLAIN ISLANDS

Unfolding like a forgotten ribbon just north of Burlington are the Champlain Islands, a 27-mile-long stretch of three largely undeveloped isles – South Hero, North Hero and Isle La Motte – all connected by US 2 and a series of bridges and causeways. It's an easy day trip from Burlington, perfect for aimless meandering. Below are a few highlights.

Allenholm Orchards (www.allenholm.com; 111 South St, South Hero; ⊙9am-5pm late May–Christmas Eve; 🚼) Pick-your-own apples, plus a petting zoo and playground for kids.

Grand Isle State Park (www.vtstateparks.com/htm/grandisle.htm; Grand Isle; tent & RV sites $20, lean-tos/cabins $27/48; ⊙May–mid-Oct) Waterfront living in four cabins, 36 lean-tos and 117 tent/trailer sites.

Hyde Log Cabin (☑802-828-3051; 228 US2, Grand Isle; adult/child $3/free; ⊙11am-5pm Sat Sun Jul–mid-Oct) One of the oldest (1783) log cabins in the US.

Hero's Welcome (www.heroswelcome.com; 3537 Hwy 2, North Hero; ⊙6:30am-6:30pm Mon-Sat, 7am-6pm Sun) A quirky, jam-packed general store with a good deli and dockside seating out front.

North Hero House (☑802-372-4732; www.northherohouse.com; 3643 US2, North Hero; r from $140; 🐾) A country inn with incomparable, front-row lake views of the water and a fantastic restaurant, **Steamship Pier Bar & Grill** (sandwiches $10-20; ⊙5-8pm Thu-Sat), serving kebabs, burgers, lobster rolls and cocktails on the pier.

Northeast Kingdom

When Senator George Aiken noted in 1949 that 'this is such beautiful country up here. It ought to be called the Northeast Kingdom of Vermont,' locals were quick to take his advice. Today, the Northeast Kingdom connotes the large wedge between the Quebec and New Hampshire borders. Less spectacular than spectacularly unspoiled, the landscape is a sea of green hills, with the occasional small village and farm spread out in the distance.

Here, inconspicuous inns and dairy cows contrast with the slick resorts and Morgan horses of the southern part of the state; the white steeples are chipped, the barns in need of a fresh coat of paint. In a rural state known for its unpopulated setting (only Wyoming contains fewer people), the Kingdom is Vermont's equivalent to putting on its finest pastoral dress, with a few holes here and there. It's a region that doesn't put on any airs about attracting tourists, and locals speak wryly of its 'picturesque poverty.'

While St Johnsbury is easily reached by I-91 or I-93 (a three-hour drive from Boston through New Hampshire), the rest of the Northeast Kingdom is spread out. Use I-91 as your north–south thoroughfare, and then use smaller routes like VT 5A to find dramatically sited Lake Willoughby, or VT 14 to find picturesque Craftsbury Common.

⊙ Sights

St Johnsbury Athenaeum   MUSEUM
(☑802-748-8291; www.stjathenaeum.org; 1171 Main St, St Johnsbury; ⊙10am-5:30pm Mon-Fri, to 3pm Sat) **FREE** Home to the country's oldest art gallery still in its original form, the athenaeum was initially founded as a library by Horace Fairbanks in 1871. Comprising some 9000 finely bound books of classic world literature, the library was soon complemented by the gallery, built around its crown jewel, Albert Bierstadt's 10ft-by-15ft painting, *Domes of the Yosemite.* The collection also includes other large-scale dramatic landscapes by Bierstadt's fellow Hudson River School artists such as Asher B Durand, Worthington Whittredge and Jasper Crospey.

Fairbanks Museum & Planetarium   MUSEUM
(☑802-748-2372; www.fairbanksmuseum.org; 1302 Main St, St Johnsbury; adult/child & senior $8/6; ⊙9am-5pm Mon-Sat, 1-5pm Sun, closed Mon Nov-Mar) In 1891, when Franklin Fairbanks' collection of stuffed animals and cultural artifacts from across the globe grew too large for his home, he built the Fairbanks Museum of Natural Science. This massive building with a 30ft-high barrel-vaulted ceiling displays more than half of Franklin's original collection, including a 1200lb moose, a Bengal tiger and a bizarre

collection of 'mosaics' made entirely from dead bugs. The attached planetarium offers **shows** ($5 per person) throughout the year.

Activities

Not surprisingly, this sylvan countryside is the perfect playground for New England outdoor activities, including skiing, mountain biking and boating.

On VT 114 off I-91, East Burke is a terrific place to start a mountain-bike ride.

Jay Peak SKIING
(☎802-988-2611; www.jaypeakresort.com; VT 242, Jay) Even when Boston is balmy, you can still expect a blizzard at Vermont's northernmost ski resort, only 10 miles south of the Quebec border. Jay gets more snow than any other ski area in New England (about 350in of powder). The mountain has plenty of easy and intermediate runs, but also offers some of America's most challenging backcountry snowboarding and skiing.

Craftsbury Outdoor Center SKIING
(☎802-586-7767; www.craftsbury.com; 535 Lost Nation Rd, Craftsbury Common; ☀) Cross-country skiers adore this full-service resort just outside the village of Craftsbury Common, 38 miles northwest of St Johnsbury. The 80 miles of trails – 50 of them groomed – roll over meadows and weave through forests of maple and fir, offering an ideal experience for all levels. In summer, the center is also a mecca for runners and boaters.

★ **Kingdom Trails** CYCLING
(www.kingdomtrails.com; day passes adult/child $15/7, year-round passes $75; ☀) ✎ In the summer of 1997 a group of dedicated locals linked together more than 200 miles of single and double tracks and dirt roads to form this astounding, award-winning trail network. Riding on a soft forest floor dusted with pine needles and through century-old farms makes for one of the best mountain-biking experiences in New England. Passes can be purchased at the **Kingdom Trails Welcome Center** (478 VT 114, East Burke; ☀8am-5pm Sun-Thu, to 6pm Fri & Sat).

East Burke Sports BICYCLE RENTAL
(☎802-626-3215; www.eastburkesports.com; 439 VT 114, East Burke; bicycles per day from $30; ☀9am-6pm) Supplies maps and rents bikes, including top-of-the-line models for serious mountain bikers.

Hiking

The stunning beauty of **Lake Willoughby** will leave even a jaded visitor in awe. The lake sits sandwiched between Mt Hor and Mt Pisgah, where the cliffs plummet more than 1000ft to the glacial waters below and create, in essence, a landlocked fjord.

The scenery is best appreciated on the hike (three hours) to the summit of **Mt Pisgah**. From West Burke, take VT 5A for 6 miles to a parking area on the left-hand side of the road, just south of Lake Willoughby. The 1.7-mile (one way) **South Trail** begins across the highway. It's about a 35-minute drive from St Johnsbury.

🛏 Sleeping

Rodgers Country Inn INN $
(☎800-729-1704, 802-525-6677; 582 Rodgers Rd, West Glover; d incl breakfast from $80, cabins per week $600) Not far from the shores of Shadow Lake, Jim and Nancy Rodgers offer five guest rooms in their 1840s farmhouse, plus two independent cabins. Hang out on the front porch and read, or take a stroll on this 350-acre former dairy farm. This inn appeals to people who really want to feel what it's like to live in rural Vermont.

★ **Inn at Mountain View Farm** INN $$
(☎800-572-4509, 802-626-9924; www.innmtnview.com; 3383 Darling Hill Rd, East Burke; r/ste incl breakfast $175/275; ☎) Built in 1883 this spacious, elegant farmhouse is set on a hilltop with stunning views, surrounded by 440 acres that are ideal for mountain biking,

Mountain biking, Kingdom Trails
FRANZ MARC FREI/GETTY IMAGES ©

cross-country skiing or simply taking a long stroll on the hillside. There's also an on-site animal sanctuary, which is a rescue center for large farm animals; guests are encouraged to visit.

Eating

Miss Lyndonville Diner DINER $
(☑802-626-9890; 686 Broad St/US 5, Lyndonville; mains $5-12; ☺6am-8pm Mon-Thu, 6am-9pm Fri & Sat, 7am-8pm Sun) Five miles north of St Johnsbury and popular with locals, this place offers friendly, prompt service and a tantalizing display of pies. Large breakfasts are cheap, as are the sandwiches, but for a real steal try the tasty homemade dinners like roast turkey with all the fixings.

Trout River Brewery BREWERY, PIZZERIA $$
(☑802-626-9396; www.troutriverbrewing.com; Hwy 5, Lyndonville; pizzas from $12; ☺4-9pm Fri & Sat) This roadside artisanal brewery is a great hangout on Friday and Saturday nights, when pints of beer are accompanied by gourmet sourdough pizzas; one local classic is Smokin' Hot Trout, with smoked trout, dill, scallions and capers.

River Garden Cafe INTERNATIONAL $$$
(☑802-626-3514; www.rivergardencafe.com; 427 Main St/VT 114, East Burke; mains $15-27; ☺11:30am-2pm & 5-9pm Wed-Sun) A summer patio within earshot of the river and a back-porch dining area that's open year-round set a mood of casual elegance at this popular eatery. The wide-ranging menu includes chicken marsala, filet mignon, rainbow trout, lamb chops, duck breast and steaks, along with pasta dishes and salads. Don't miss the cinnamon rolls at Sunday brunch.

ⓘ Information

Northeast Kingdom Chamber of Commerce
(☑802-748-3678; www.nekchamber.com; Ste 11, 2000 Memorial Dr, St Johnsbury; ☺8:30am-5pm mid-Jun–mid-Oct) Plentiful regional information, 3 miles north of town in the Green Mountain Mall just off US 5.

ⓘ Getting There & Away

To get to St Johnsbury from Montpelier (55 minutes, 38 miles), take US 2 east; from Burlington, I-89 to US 2 (1½ hours, 76 miles). To get to Brattleboro (two hours, 122 miles), take a straight shot south down I-91. The only way to get around the Northeast Kingdom is with your own wheels.

Central Vermont

Nestled in the Green Mountains, central Vermont is classic small-town, big-countryside New England. Its picturesque villages and venerable ski resorts have been luring travelers for generations.

Woodstock & Quechee

The archetypal Vermont town, Woodstock has streets lined with graceful Federal- and Georgian-style houses. The Ottauquechee River, spanned by a covered bridge, meanders right through the heart of town. Quechee (*kwee*-chee), 7 miles to the northeast, is famous for its dramatic gorge, dubbed 'Vermont's Little Grand Canyon.'

◉ Sights

★**Quechee Gorge** CANYON
FREE Quechee Gorge, an impressive 163ft-deep, 3000ft-long chasm cut by the Ottauquechee River, can be viewed from above or explored via nearby walking trails. The adjacent **visitor center** (5966 Woodstock Rd; ☺9am-5pm) has trail maps and local information

★**VINS Nature Center** RAPTOR CENTER
(☑802-359-5000; www.vinsweb.org; 6565 Woodstock Rd; adult/child 4-17yr $13.50/11.50; ☺10am-5pm mid-Apr–Oct, to 4pm Nov–mid-Apr ; ☕) ✿ You may feel like ducking during the live raptor show when several magnificent raptors show off their mad flight skills. Visit this nature center, a mile west of Quechee Gorge, for a close-up look at bald eagles, snow owls, and red-tailed hawks. More than 40 raptors are rehabilitated here.

Marsh-Billings-Rockefeller National Historical Park PARK
(☑802-457-3368; www.nps.gov/mabi; 53 Elm St, Woodstock; mansion tours adult/child under 16yr $8/free, trails free; ☺visitor center 10am-5pm late May-Oct, tours every 30min) Encompassing the historic home and estate of early American conservationist George Perkins Marsh, Vermont's only national park offers mansion tours on the hour, plus 20 miles of trails and carriage roads for walkers, cross-country skiers and snowshoers. Advance reservations are recommended for tours. Specialty tours may be substituted for the mansion tour on certain days, so call ahead to confirm which tour is being offered.

Billings Farm & Museum FARM

(📞802-457-2355; www.billingsfarm.org; 69 Old River Rd, Woodstock; adult/child 5-15yr/child 3-4yr $14/8/4; ⏰10am-5pm daily May-Oct, to 3.30pm Sat & Sun Nov-Feb; 🚗) 🐾 A mile north of the village green, this historic farm delights children with its pretty Jersey cows and hands-on demonstrations of traditional farm life. Family-friendly seasonal events include wagon and sleigh rides, a pumpkin and apple festival, and old-fashioned Halloween, Thanksgiving and Christmas celebrations.

🛏️ Sleeping

Quechee State Park CAMPGROUND $

(📞802-295-2990; www.vtstateparks.com/htm/ quechee.htm; 5800 Woodstocck Rd/US 4, Quechee; tent & RV sites/lean-tos from $20/25; ⏰mid-May–mid-Oct) Perched on the edge of Quechee Gorge, this 611-acre spot has 45 pine-shaded campsites and seven lean-tos.

Ardmore Inn B&B $$

(📞802-457-3887; www.ardmoreinn.com; 23 Pleasant St, Woodstock; r incl breakfast $219-259; ❄️📶) Congenial owners and lavish breakfasts enhance the considerable appeal of this stately, centrally located 1867 Victorian–Greek Revival inn with five antique-laden rooms.

Shire Riverview Motel MOTEL $$

(📞802-457-2211; www.shiremotel.com; 46 Pleasant St/US 4, Woodstock; r $149-209; ❄️📶) Spring the extra few dollars for a river view at this 42-room motel, which features a wrap-around porch overlooking the Ottauquechee River. Expect classic, not-too-fancy decor and a few country prints.

🍴 Eating

Mon Vert Cafe CAFE $

(📞802-457-7143; www.monvertcafe.com; 67 Central St; breakfast $6-13, lunch $9-11; ⏰7:30am-5pm Mon-Thu, to 6pm Fri & Sat) Pop into this bright and airy cafe for croissants, scones, and egg sandwiches in the morning, or settle in on the patio for salads and panini at lunch. Enjoy the maple latte anytime. Ingredients are sourced locally, and farms and food purveyors are listed on the wall.

Melaza Caribbean Bistro PUERTO RICAN $$

(📞802-457-7110; www.melazabistro.com; 71 Central St; small plates $5-12, mains $16-25; ⏰5:30-8:30 Sun, Wed & Thu, to 9pm Fri & Sat) Service was a little too casual on our visit, but all was forgiven after the first bite of the perfectly seasoned rice and chicken *sofrito*, served with avocados and *brava* (spicy tomato) sauce. Unwind here after day of exploring, with a glass of wine and an enticing mix of Puerto Rican and tropically inspired tapas and entrees.

⭐Simon Pearce Restaurant NEW AMERICAN $$$

(📞802-295-1470; www.simonpearce.com; 1760 Main St, Quechee; lunch $13-19, dinner $22-38; ⏰11:30am-2:45pm & 5:30-9pm Mon-Sat, 10:30am-2:45 & 5:30-9pm Sun) Reserve ahead for a window-side table suspended over the river in this converted brick mill, where fresh-from-the-farm local ingredients are used to inventive effect. The restaurant's beautiful stemware is blown by hand in the Simon Pearce Glass workshops next door. The Vermont cheddar soup is always a good choice.

ℹ️ Information

Woodstock Area Chamber of Commerce Welcome Center (📞802-432-1100; www.woodstockvt.com; Mechanic St, Woodstock; ⏰9am-5pm) On a riverside backstreet, two blocks from the village green.

Killington

A half-hour's drive west of Woodstock, **Killington Resort** (📞802-422-6200; www.killington.com; adult/senior/child 7-18yr lift ticket weekend $92/78/71, midweek $84/71/65) boasts one of the East's longest ski seasons. Out of season, mountain bikers and hikers claim the slopes. **K-1 Lodge** boasts the Express Gondola, which transports up to 3000 skiers per hour in heated cars along a 2.5-mile cable and is the highest lift in Vermont.

Killington is jam-packed with accommodations, from cozy ski lodges to chain hotels. Most are along Killington Rd, the 6-mile road that heads up the mountain from US 4. The **Killington Chamber of Commerce** (📞802-773-4181; www.killingtonchamber.com; 2319 US 4, Killington; ⏰10am-5pm Mon-Fri, to 2pm Sat) has all the nitty-gritty.

Middlebury

Standing at the nexus of several state highways, aptly named Middlebury was built along the falls of Otter Creek at the end of the 18th century. In 1800 Middlebury College was founded, and it has been synonymous with the town ever since. Poet Robert Frost (1874–1963) owned a farm in nearby Ripton and co-founded the college's renowned Bread Loaf School of English in the hills above town. The college is also famous for its summer foreign-language programs, which have been drawing linguists here for nearly a century. Middlebury's history of marble quarrying is evident in the college's architecture: many buildings are made with white marble and gray limestone.

◉ Sights

University of Vermont
Morgan Horse Farm FARM
(☑802-388-2011; www.uvm.edu/morgan; 74 Battell Dr, Weybridge; adult/child $5/2; ⊙9am-4pm May-Oct; ⊕) See registered Morgan horses and tour their stables at this farm 3 miles north of Middlebury. Known for their strength, agility, endurance and longevity, and named after Justin Morgan, who brought his thoroughbred Arabian colt to Vermont in 1789, these little horses became America's first native breed, useful for heavy work, carriage draft, riding and even war service.

Otter Creek Brewing BREWERY
(☑802-388-0727; www.ottercreekbrewing.com; 793 Exchange St; ⊙11am-6pm) One of New England's best, this brewery makes several fine craft beers, including its trademark Copper Ale, Stovepipe Porter and the organic Wolaver's line. Stop by for a pint and a bite at the recently opened brewpub.

Champlain Orchards FARM
See p30.

Middlebury College
Museum of Art MUSEUM
(☑802-443-5007; http://museum.middlebury.edu; 72 Porter Field Rd; ⊙10am-5pm Tue-Fri, noon-5pm Sat & Sun) **FREE** Small but diverse museum with rotating exhibitions alongside a fine permanent collection that includes an Egyptian sarcophagus, Cypriot pottery, 19th-century European and American sculpture, and works by such luminaries as Pablo Picasso, Salvador Dalí, Alice Neel and Andy Warhol.

⚑ Activities

Undulating with rolling hills and farms, the pastoral countryside around Middlebury makes for great cycling. Nearby Green Mountain National Forest is also home to some great ski areas.

Middlebury College Snow Bowl SKIING
(☑802-443-7669; 6886 VT 125; ⊙9am-4pm Mon-Fri, 8:30am-4pm Sat & Sun; ⊕) One of Vermont's most affordable, least crowded ski

areas, this college-owned facility has only three lifts, but with trails for all levels, nonexistent lift lines, and prices half of what you'd pay elsewhere, who's complaining? Middlebury's 'graduation on skis' takes place here each February: graduates slalom down the slopes in full valedictory regalia, their dark robes fluttering amid the snowflakes.

⊨ Sleeping

Branbury State Park CAMPGROUND $
(☑802-247-5925; www.vtstateparks.com/branbury.htm; VT 53; campsite/lean-to $20/27; ⊙late May–mid-Oct; ⊕) Ten miles south of Middlebury at the foot of the Green Mountains, this family-friendly 96-acre lakeside park has 37 campsites and seven lean-tos. The small beach, which offers swimming and rental boats, is backed by a grassy lawn with playground and barbecue facilities. Hiking trails climb to the pretty Falls of Lana and Silver Lake in Green Mountain National Forest.

Inn on the Green INN $$
(☑888-244-7512, 802-388-7512; www.innonthegreen.com; 71 S Pleasant St; r incl breakfast $159-299; ✲◉☎) Lovingly restored to its original stateliness, this 1803 Federal-style home has spacious rooms in the main house and in an adjoining carriage house (where the rooms are more modern). One of its signature treats is breakfast served in bed each morning.

Waybury Inn INN $$
(☑800-348-1810, 802-388-4015; www.wayburyinn.com; VT 125, East Middlebury; r/ste incl breakfast from $130/280; ☎) A favorite of Robert Frost, this former stagecoach stop 5 miles southeast of Middlebury has a wood-paneled restaurant and sumptuous guest rooms. The inn's exterior was featured in the 1980s TV

show *Newhart* (though Bob's never actually been here). Laze away a summer afternoon in the nearby swimming hole or warm yourself in the pub on a wintry evening.

Swift House Inn   INN $$
(☎ 866-388-9925; www.swifthouseinn.com; 25 Stewart Lane; r incl breakfast $139-279; ☎) Two blocks north of the town green, this grand white Federal mansion (1814) is surrounded by fine formal lawns and gardens. Luxurious standard rooms in the main house and adjacent carriage house are supplemented by suites that have fireplaces, sitting areas and Jacuzzis. Other welcome luxuries include a steam room and sauna, a cozy pub, a library and a sun porch.

Middlebury Inn   INN $$
(☎ 800-842-4666, 802-388-4961; www.middlebury inn.com; 14 Court Sq, VT 7; r $139-279; ☎) Directly opposite the town green, this inn's fine old main building (1827) has beautifully restored formal public rooms with wide hallways, and its charming guest rooms have all the modern conveniences. The adjacent Porter Mansion, with Victorian-style rooms, is also full of attractive architectural details. Lower-priced units in the modern annex out back are considerably less appealing.

✖ Eating & Drinking

Middlebury Bagel & Deli   BAKERY $
(11 Washington St; breakfast $5-9; ☺ 6am-2pm Mon-Fri) Since 1979 the Rubright family has been showing up at 4am daily to bake some of New England's finest doughnuts and bagels. Skiers on their way to the slopes, workers en route to the job site and professors headed for class all converge here for warm-from-the-oven apple fritters, doughnuts and bagels, along with omelets and other breakfast treats.

★ American Flatbread   PIZZERIA $$
(☎ 802-388-3300; americanflatbread.com; 137 Maple St; flatbreads $14-20; ☺ 5-9pm Tue-Fri, noon-9pm Sat) 🅿 In a cavernous old marble building with a blazing fire that keeps things cozy in winter, this is one of Middlebury's most beloved eateries. The menu is limited to farm-fresh salads and custom-made flatbreads (don't call it pizza or they'll come after you with the paddle) topped with locally sourced organic cheeses, meat and veggies, accompanied by Vermont microbrews on tap.

51 Main   INTERNATIONAL $$
(☎ 802-388-8209; www.go51main.com; 51 Main St; mains $12-24; ☺ 4pm-late Tue-Sat; ☎) Overlook-

ing Otter Creek, this high-ceilinged restaurant, lounge and live-music venue was started by a few Middlebury College students as a fun social space where people could dine, perform and generally hang out. It features a convivial, casual bar and serves an eclectic international menu: Brazilian shrimp stew, cider-glazed pork chops and gourmet mac-and-fromage – made with Vermont cheddar, of course.

Storm Cafe   CAFE $$
(☎ 802-388-1063; www.thestormcafe.com; 3 Mill St; mains $12-25; ☺ 11am-2:30pm Tue-Fri, 9am-2pm Sat & Sun, dinner 5pm-close Wed-Sat) In the basement of Frog Hollow Mill, this creekside cafe serves breakfast, followed by soups, salads and sandwiches at lunchtime. In good weather, the more substantial dinner offerings are best enjoyed out on the terrace overlooking the falls of Otter Creek; some consider this to be the most imaginative menu in town.

❶ Information

Addison County Chamber of Commerce (☎ 802-388-7951; www.addisoncounty.com; 93 Court St) About half a mile south of the town green, this place dispenses plenty of information.

Green Mountain National Forest District Office (☎ 802-388-4362; 1007 US 7; ☺ 8am-4:30pm Mon-Fri) Drop by this ranger station 2 miles south of town for information about the many good day hikes in the region.

❶ Getting There & Away

Middlebury is right on US 7. To get here from Burlington (50 minutes, 35 miles), take US 7 south; from Manchester (1½ hours, 65 miles), take US 7 or VT 30 north.

Southern Vermont

The southern swath of Vermont holds the state's oldest towns and plenty of scenic back roads.

Brattleboro

The counterculture of the 1960s is alive and well in this riverside burg overflowing with artsy types and more tie-dye per capita than any other place in New England.

◉ Sights

Paralleling the Connecticut River, Main St is lined with period buildings, including the handsome art-deco **Latchis Building**. The surrounding area boasts several **covered bridges**; pick up a map at the Bennington Chamber of Commerce.

Brattleboro Museum & Art Center MUSEUM
(www.brattleboromuseum.org; 10 Vernon St; adult/student/child under 18yr $8/4/free; ☺11am-5pm Wed-Mon) Located in a 1915 railway station, this museum hosts rotating exhibitions of contemporary art, including multimedia works by local artists.

🛏 Sleeping

If all you're after is a cheap sleep, there are plenty of motels on Putney Rd north of town; take Exit 3 off I-91.

Latchis Hotel HOTEL **$$**
(☎802-254-6300, 800-798-6301; www.latchis.com; 50 Main St; r incl breakfast $115-170, ste $185; ☎) The decor is retro and your view from an interior room may be a redbrick wall, but this art-deco hotel has charm. And you can't beat the prime downtown location and the attached historic theater.

Forty Putney Road B&B B&B **$$$**
(☎800-941-2413, 802-254-6268; www.fortyputneyroad.com; 192 Putney Rd; r incl breakfast $159-329; @☎) In a sweet riverside location just north of town, this 1930 B&B has a cheery pub, a pool table, a hot tub, a glorious backyard, four rooms and a separate self-contained cottage. Easy access to river trails from the property.

🍴 Eating

Brattleboro Food Co-op DELI **$**
(☎802-257-0236; www.brattleborofoodcoop.com; 2 Main St; sandwiches $7-9; ☺7am-9pm Mon-Sat, 9am-9pm Sun) 🌿 At this thriving downtown community market, load up your basket with wholefood groceries, organic produce, and local cheeses, or visit the juice bar and deli for healthy takeaway treats.

Whetstone Station PUB **$$**
(☎802-490-2354; www.whetstonestation.com; 36 Bridge St; mains $10-22; ☺11:30am-10pm Sun-Thu, to 11pm Fri & Sat) At sunset, dine on the deck overlooking the Connecticut River for one of the finest views in town. This busy brewery and eatery has 20 or so craft beers on tap – with house and guest brewery selections – plus a wide range of craft bottles and cans. For a light but filling meal, try the grilled sirloin tips with a dipping sauce. Fantastic! Welcoming service, too.

TJ Buckley's AMERICAN **$$$**
(☎802-257-4922; www.tjbuckleys.com; 132 Elliot St; mains $40; ☺5:30-9pm Thu-Sun) 🌿 Chef-owner Michael Fuller founded this exceptional, upscale 18-seat eatery in an authentic 1927 diner over 30 years ago. The oral menu of four nightly changing items is sourced largely from local organic farms. Reserve ahead.

ℹ Information

Brattleboro Chamber of Commerce (☎877-254-4565, 802-254-4565; www.brattleborochamber.org; 180 Main St; ☺9am-5pm Mon-Fri) Stop by for a free historical society walking-tour map.

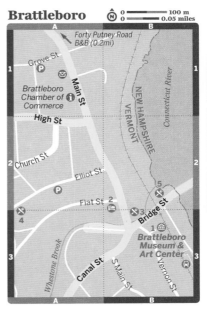

Brattleboro 🅝 0 ___ 100 m / 0 ___ 0.05 miles

VERMONT SOUTHERN VERMONT

Bennington

Southern Vermont is rural, and cozy Bennington, with about 15,000 inhabitants, ranks as the region's largest town. An interesting mix of cafes and shops downtown line Main St, while the adjacent Old Bennington historic district boasts Colonial homes, the early 19th-century Old First Church, where poet Robert Frost is buried, and a trio of covered bridges. A hilltop granite obelisk commemorating the 1777 Battle of Bennington towers above it all.

◉ Sights

Bennington Battle Monument   HISTORIC SITE
(www.benningtonbattlemonument.com; 15 Monument Circle; adult/child 6-14yr $5/1; ⊘9am-5pm mid-Apr–Oct) This striking structure, which rises more than 300ft, offers an unbeatable 360-degree view of the surrounding countryside. An elevator whisks you painlessly to the top.

Bennington Museum   MUSEUM
(☑802-447-1571; www.benningtonmuseum.org; 75 Main St; adult/child under 18yr $10/free; ⊘10am-5pm daily, closed Jan, closed Wed Nov-Jun) Between downtown and Old Bennington, this museum houses an outstanding early Americana collection which includes Bennington pottery, and the Bennington Flag (one of the oldest surviving American Revolutionary flags), and works by American folk artist 'Grandma Moses.'

🛏 Sleeping & Eating

**Greenwood Lodge
& Campsites**   HOSTEL, CAMPGROUND $
(☑802-442-2547; www.campvermont.com/greenwood; VT 9, Prospect Mountain; 2-person tent/RV site $29/35, dm $30-36, private room 1/2 people $72/75; ⊘mid-May–late Oct; 🐾) Nestled in the Green Mountains 8 miles east of town, this 120-acre space with three ponds holds one of Vermont's best-sited hostels and campgrounds.

Henry House   B&B $$
(☑802-442-7045; www.thehenryhouseinn.com; 1338 Murphy Rd, North Bennington; r incl breakfast $100-155; 🐾) Sit on the rocking chair and watch the traffic trickle across a covered bridge at this Colonial home on 25 peaceful acres, built in 1769 by American Revolutionary hero William Henry.

Blue Benn Diner   DINER $
(☑802-442-5140; 314 North St; mains $7-16; ⊘6am-4:45pm Mon-Fri, 7am-3:45pm Sat & Sun; 🐾) This classic 1950s-era diner serves breakfast all day and a healthy mix of American and international fare. Enhancing the retro experience are little tabletop jukeboxes where you can play Willie Nelson's 'Moonlight in Vermont' till your neighbors scream for mercy. Cash only.

Pangaea   INTERNATIONAL $$$
(☑802-442-7171; www.vermontfinedining.com; 1 Prospect St, North Bennington; lounge mains from $10-23, restaurant mains $30; ⊘lounge from 5pm daily, restaurant 5-9pm Tue-Sat) Offering fine dining for every budget, this top-end North Bennington restaurant sits side-by-side with a more casual, intimate lounge. Opt for gourmet burgers served on the riverside terrace out back, or head to the tastefully decorated dining room next door for international specialties such as filet mignon on risotto, topped with pancetta and taleggio.

❶ Information

Bennington Area Chamber of Commerce
(☑802-447-331; www.bennington.com; 100 Veterans Memorial Dr; ⊘10am-5pm Mon-Fri) One mile north of downtown. The chamber also runs the Bennington Welcome Center (100 Route 279, 7am to 9pm), near the Rte 279 and US 7 interchange, which is open daily .

Old First Church, Bennington
JOHN ELK/GETTY IMAGES ©

VERMONT

SCENIC DRIVE: COVERED BRIDGES OF BENNINGTON

North of Bennington, a 30-minute detour takes you across three picture-perfect covered bridges spanning the Wallomsac River. To get started, turn west onto VT 67A just north of Bennington's tourist office and continue 3.5 miles, bearing left on Murphy Rd at the 117ft-long **Burt Henry Covered Bridge** (1840). After curving to the left, Murphy Rd next loops through the **Paper Mill Bridge**, which takes its name from the 1790 mill whose gear works are still visible along the river below. Next turn right onto VT 67A, go half a mile and turn right onto Silk Rd where you'll soon cross the **Silk Road Bridge** (c 1840). Continue southeast for two more miles, bearing left at two T-intersections, to reach the **Bennington Battle Monument** (p106).

Manchester

Sitting in the shadow of Mt Equinox, Manchester's been a fashionable summer retreat since the 19th century. The mountain scenery, the agreeable climate and the Batten Kill River – Vermont's best trout stream – continue to draw vacationers today. Manchester Center, at the town's north end, sports cafes and upscale outlet stores. Further south lies dignified Manchester Village, lined with marble sidewalks, stately homes and the posh Equinox hotel.

Manchester's a terrific base from which to visit quintessential towns such as Dorset.

◉ Sights & Activities

The **Appalachian Trail**, which overlaps the **Long Trail** in southern Vermont, passes just east of Manchester. For trail maps and details on shorter day hikes, stop by the **Green Mountain National Forest office** (802-362-2307; www.fs.usda.gov/greenmountain; 2538 Depot St, Manchester Center; 8am-4:30pm Mon-Fri).

★ Hildene   HISTORIC SITE
(802-362-1788, 800-578-1788; www.hildene.org; 1005 Hildene Rd/VT 7A; adult/child 6-14yr $16/5; guided tours $5/2; 9:30am-4:30pm) This stately 24-room Georgian revival mansion was home to members of Abraham Lincoln's family from the 1800s until 1975, when it was converted into a museum. The collection of family heirlooms includes the hat Lincoln probably wore while delivering the Gettysburg Address – one of the three surviving Lincoln top hats. The gorgeous grounds offer 12 miles of walking and cross-country ski trails.

**American Museum of
Fly Fishing & Orvis**   MUSEUM
(www.amff.com; 4070 Main St; adult/child 5-14yr $5/3; 10am-4pm Tue-Sun Jun-Oct, Tue-Sat Nov-May) In this small museum, check out fly-fishing gear once owned by America's manliest men, including Ernest Hemingway, Babe Ruth, Zane Grey and former president George Bush. Another exhibit traces the history of trout fishing and fly fishing.

Skyline Drive   SCENIC DRIVE
(802-362-1114; www.equinoxmountain.com; car & driver $15, extra passenger $5; 9am-5pm late May-Oct, cars admitted until 4pm) For spectacular views, drive to the summit of **Mt Equinox** (3816ft) via Skyline Drive, a private 5-mile toll road off VT 7A.

🛏 Sleeping & Eating

Aspen Motel   MOTEL $
(802-362-2450; www.theaspenatmanchester.com; 5669 Main St/VT 7A; r $85-150; ❋❄🐾🖥) Rhododendrons and other bright flowers set a pretty stage at this family-run motel set back serenely from the road. The 24-room motel is within walking distance of Manchester Center.

Inn at Manchester   INN $$
(802-362-1793, 800-273-1793; www.innatmanchester.com; 3967 Main St/VT 7A; r/ste incl breakfast from $165/255; ❋@🐾🖥) The hospitality is what you notice first at this delightful inn and carriage house in the heart of downtown. Relax in comfy rooms with quilts and country furnishings, or step out your door for the big front porch, afternoon teas, an expansive backyard and a wee pub.

Spiral Press Café   CAFE $
(802-362-9944; cnr VT 11 & VT 7A; mains $8-10; 7:30am-7pm Mon-Sat, 8:30-7pm Sun; 🐾) Attached to the fabulous Northshire Bookstore, Manchester Center's favorite cafe draws locals and tourists with good coffee, tasty cookies, flaky croissants and delicious sandwiches.

Ye Olde Tavern   AMERICAN $$$
(802-362-0611; www.yeoldetavern.net; 5183 Main St; mains $18-35; 5-9pm) At this gracious roadside 1790s inn, hearthside dining at candlelit tables enhances the wide-ranging

menu of 'Yankee favorites' such as traditional pot roast (cooked in the tavern's own ale) or local venison (a Friday evening special).

ℹ Information

Manchester and the Mountains Regional Chamber of Commerce (☑ 802-362-6313; www.visitmanchestervt.com; 39 Bonnet St, Manchester Center; ☺ 9am-5pm Mon-Fri, 10am-3pm Sat, 11am-3pm Sun; ☎) Spiffy office with free wi-fi.

Dorset

Six miles northwest of Manchester along VT 30, Dorset is a pristinely beautiful Vermont village, originally settled in 1768, with a stately inn (the oldest in Vermont), a lofty church and a village green. The sidewalks and many buildings are made of creamy marble from the nearby **quarry**, about a mile south of the village center on VT 30. Dorset supplied much of the marble for the grand New York Public Library building and numerous other public edifices. These days the quarry is filled with water and makes a lovely place to picnic. Dorset is best known as a summer playground for well-to-do city folks (a role it has played for over a century) and is the home of renowned theater the **Dorset Playhouse** (☑ 802-867-5777; www.dorsetplayers.org; 104 Cheney Rd).

Vermont's oldest continuously operating inn (in business since 1796), the **Dorset Inn** (☑ 802-867-5500; www.dorsetinn.com; 8 Church St; r incl breakfast $165-475; ☎) is still going strong. Just off VT 30 facing the village green, this traditional but plush inn has 35 guest rooms and suites, some with fireplaces and Jacuzzis. The front-porch rockers provide a nice setting for watching the comings and goings of this sleepy Vermont town. The on-site **restaurant** (mains $15-29), serving bistro food and locally sourced items, is highly regarded, or pop into the spa for some pampering.

Innkeepers Jean and Jim Kingston greet travelers at the tidy 1800s **Dovetail Inn** (☑ 802-867-5747, 888-867-5747; www.dovetailinn.com; VT 30; r incl continental breakfast $99-265; ✳ ☎), which faces the village green. Breakfast is served in the comfort of the 11 well-kept guest rooms across two houses.

Dorset Union Store (☑ 802-867-4400; 31 Church St; ☺ 7am-6pm Mon-Thu & Sun, to 7pm Fri & Sat) sells all manner of edible Vermont items, especially high-end gourmet goodies and picnic fixings, including cheese (of course); it also has a well-stocked wine room, a deli and a freezer full of gourmet take-and-bake treats, including its award-winning mac-and-cheese.

Newfane

Vermont is rife with pretty villages, but Newfane is near the top of everyone's list. All the postcard-perfect sights you'd expect in a Vermont town are here: tall old trees, white high-steepled churches, adorable inns and gracious old houses. A short stroll exposes Newfane's core: you'll see the stately **Congregational Church** (1839), the **Windham County Courthouse** (1825), built in Greek Revival style, and a few antique shops.

Newfane is on VT 30, just 12 miles northwest of Brattleboro and 19 miles northeast of Wilmington.

Grafton

The must-see village of Grafton is graceful, and it's not that way by accident. In the 1960s the private Windham Foundation established a restoration and preservation program for the entire village, and it has been eminently successful. The foundation's initiatives included burying all electrical and telephone lines, which helps account for Grafton's ultra-picturesque, lost-in-time appearance.

In the heart of the village, visit the retail shop of local success story, Grafton Village Cheese Company, **MKT Grafton** (☑ 802-843-2255; www.mktgrafton.com; 56 Townshend Rd; ☺ 10am-5pm Sat-Thu, 11am-6pm Fri) which offers free samples of Grafton's many mouth-watering, nose-tingling cheddar varieties, which you can also purchase here along with wine and beer. The maple-smoked and stone-house cheddars regularly win awards at international cheese festivals. Tours of the actual cheese-production facility, half a mile down the street at 533 Townshend Rd, are sometimes available; ask for a schedule at the shop.

Just south of the village, **Grafton Ponds Outdoor Center** (☑ 802-843-2400; www.graftonponds.com) offers year-round recreation on mountain-biking, hiking and cross-country ski trails, along with canoeing, swimming, snow tubing and adventure camps for kids.

The double porch at **The Grafton Inn** (Old Tavern at Grafton; ☑ 802-234-8707; www.graftoninnvermont.com; 92 Main St; r/ste from $165/235; ☎) is Grafton's landmark, and the inn has played host to such notable guests as Rudyard Kipling, Theodore Roosevelt and Ralph Waldo Emerson. While the original brick inn is quite formal, many of the 45 guest rooms and suites, scattered around houses within the village, are less so. The dining room (mains $21 to $29) is New England formal, and the cuisine is refined New American with a seasonal menu. The casual on-site pub, **Phelps Barn** (www.graftoninnvermont.com/dining; ⊙4-10pm Tue-Sun), has live music every Saturday night and serves light pub food and a wide range of Vermont microbrews; or pop in for Flatbread Fridays, when it serves pizza cooked in 'Big Red,' its beloved pizza oven.

Grafton lies at the junction of VT 121 and VT 35, about 15 miles north of Newfane.

Wilmington & Mt Snow

Nestled in the upper Deerfield River valley, Wilmington is the gateway to Mt Snow, one of New England's best ski resorts and an excellent summertime mountain-biking and golfing spot. Many restaurants and stores cater to families, who are the resort's main clientele.

The state's central north–south highway, VT 100, goes north from Wilmington past Haystack and Mt Snow. Wilmington's main street is VT 9, the primary route across southern Vermont.

⊙ Sights & Activities

Mt Snow SKIING
(☏800-245-7669; www.mountsnow.com; VT 100, West Dover; adult lift ticket midweek/weekend $75/85) Southern Vermont's biggest ski resort features varied, family-friendly terrain, with 132 trails (20% beginner, 60% intermediate, 20% expert) and 23 lifts, plus a vertical drop of 1700ft and the snowmaking ability to blanket 85% of the trails. Area cross-country routes cover more than 60 miles; other winter activities include tubing and snowmobile tours.

To reach Mt Snow/Haystack from Wilmington, travel 10 miles north of town on VT 100. The free bus service **MOOver** (www.moover.com) offers free hourly transport from Wilmington to the slopes of Mt Snow between 7am and 6pm year-round, with extra services added on weekends and for the ski season.

🛏 Sleeping & Eating

Old Red Mill Inn INN $
(☏877-733-6455, 802-464-3700; www.oldredmill.com; 18 N Main St; d $65-95; 🛜) Squeezed between VT 100 and the Deerfield River's north branch, this converted sawmill in the heart of town has simple rooms (chunky wood furnishings, checkered bedspreads) at bargain prices.

Nutmeg Country Inn INN $$
(☏855-868-8634, 802-464-3907; www.nutmeginn.com; 153 W Main St, VT 9; r/ste incl breakfast from $119/209; 🛜) Just west of Wilmington, this 18th-century farmhouse has 10 rooms and four suites with antiques and reproduction pieces. Most luxurious is the Grand Deluxe King Suite, with skylights and a marble bath.

White House of Wilmington INN $$$
(☏802-464-2135; www.whitehouseinn.com; VT 9; r/ste incl breakfast from $178/350; 🛜🏊) Perched on a hillside east of town, this white Colonial Revival mansion has great cross-country trails and 16 luxury rooms, some with hot tub and fireplace. Enhancing the inn's romantic appeal are an excellent restaurant (mains $28 to $34), complete with fireplace, wood paneling and views of the Deerfield Valley; an on-site spa; and a convivial tavern.

Wahoo's Eatery AMERICAN $
(☏802-464-0010; 2 Whites Rd, VT 9; sandwiches $6-10; ⊙11am-8pm May-Sep) 'We welcome your business and relish your buns' reads the sign at this friendly, family-run roadside snack shack less than a mile east of Wilmington on VT 100. A long-standing local institution, it whips up quality burgers ($2 extra for grass-fed Vermont beef), along with hand-cut fries, handmade conch fritters, wraps, sandwiches, hot dogs, salads and ice cream.

Dot's DINER $$
(☏802-464-7284; www.dotsofvermont.com; 3 E Main St; dishes $5-16; ⊙5:30am-8pm Sun-Thu, to 9pm Fri & Sat) Devastated by flooding in 2011, Wilmington's venerable down-home diner was rebuilt from scratch and reopened in September 2013. Its spicy Jailhouse Chili, covered with melted cheese, is renowned throughout New England. With a **second location** (VT 100) in Dover, it's justly popular with locals and skiers in search of cheap sustenance like steak and eggs for breakfast.

ⓘ Information

Mt Snow Valley Chamber of Commerce (☏877-887-6884, 802-464-8092; www.visitvermont.com; 21 W Main St; ⊙8:30am-4:30pm Mon-Wed, 8:30am-6pm Thu & Fri, 10am-4pm Sat & Sun) has info on accommodations and activities.

ⓘ Getting There & Away

Wilmington is 20 miles west of Brattleboro and 20 miles east of Bennington; it's a winding half-hour drive to either town along the mountainous VT 9.

STRETCH
YOUR LEGS
STOWE

Start/Finish Quiet Path

Distance 2.5 miles

Duration Two to three hours

This walk takes you along the Quiet Path, a circular walk across bucolic farmland, and then through the center of Stowe village. You'll cross a pedestrian covered bridge, visit local galleries and shops, and learn about Stowe's skiing and snowboarding history.

Take this walk on Trip

Quiet Path

The Quiet Path is a delightful, easy 1.8-mile walk that features mountain views and takes you past bucolic farmlands along the west branch of the Little River. Along the way, special plaques explain the ecosystem of the area. The loop is blissfully devoid of cyclists or anything else that moves quickly.

The Walk » Access the walk from the parking lot beneath the church on Main St. Follow the signs to the recreation path and veer right after the second bridge. The path loops around and returns to the start. Walk up the hill, turn right at the church, then right onto Mountain Rd.

Stowe Walkway

A pedestrian covered bridge (1972), the Stowe Walkway hugs the road across the Waterbury River. One of Stowe's most photographed spots, it's a mini, skinny version of the covered bridges you see across the state and features a sweet Stowe sign at the entrance.

The Walk » Cross the pedestrian bridge. At the other end, cross the street and turn left; your next stop is on your right.

Straw Corner Shops

Stowe has no shortage of galleries and craft shops displaying work by artists of local and international renown. Within the Straw Corner Shops (Mountain Rd), offerings are traditional, contemplative, sometimes prankish and always finely hewn. Look for the Straw Corner Mercantile (☑802-253-3700; 57 Mountain Rd; ☉10am-6pm), featuring folk art, Americana, prints and artsy home accessories; and for Stowe Craft Gallery & Design Center (☑802-253-4693; www.stowecraft. com; 55 Mountain Rd; ☉10am-6pm, to 8pm Thu-Sat Jul & Aug), with adventurous, eclectic and surreal works of art and craft.

The Walk » Turn right out of the parking lot and cross Main St to the next stop, which is right across the street.

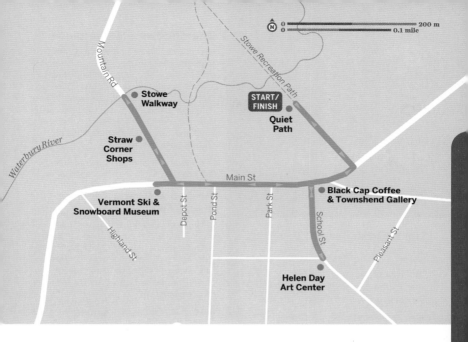

Vermont Ski & Snowboard Museum

Located in an 1818 meeting house that was rolled to its present spot by oxen in the 1860s, the Vermont Ski & Snowboard Museum (☑ 802-253-9911; www. vtssm.com; 1 S Main St; suggested donation $3-5; ⊙ noon-5pm Thu-Tue, closed Apr-late May) is a tribute to skiing and boarding, with over 7500 cataloged items. It tells the tale of the famous 10th Mountain Division of skiing troops from WWII, traces the evolution of equipment (75 years of Vermont ski lifts!) and gives you a chance to chuckle at 1970s slope-side fashion.

The Walk » Turn right out of the museum and walk down Main St — you'll pass oodles of shops and restaurants. Turn right onto School St and walk three blocks until you see your next stop on the right.

Helen Day Art Center

This gently provocative community art center (☑ 802-253-8358; www.helenday.com; School St; ⊙ noon-5pm Thu-Tue Jun–mid-Oct & Dec, Tue-Sat mid-Oct–Nov & Jan-May) hosts rotating traditional and avant-garde exhibits. It also sponsors 'Exposed,' an annual town-wide outdoor sculptural show from mid-July to mid-October.

The Walk » Walk back down School St the way you came. At Main St, the next stop is on your right at the corner.

Black Cap Coffee & Townshend Gallery

What's art without coffee? After a browse through the Townshend Gallery (featuring rotating exhibits mainly by local artists), drop into Black Cap Coffee (☑ 802-253-2123; 144 Main St; dishes $5-7; ⊙ 7am-6pm Mon-Sat, from 8am Sun; ☎) for a cuppa and a bite. It's located in an old house with a small but delightful front porch.

The Walk » To return to the beginning of the Quiet Path, cross Main St and walk down the hill (the church will be on your right) to the parking lot.

STRETCH YOUR LEGS
BURLINGTON

Start/Finish Pearl & Church Sts

Distance 3 miles

Duration Two to three hours

This walk takes you along Burlington's main drag and pedestrian hangout strip, ending with a stroll along the city's finest asset, Lake Champlain. You'll learn about the history of the city and the lake's ecosystem, and see where Burlington's outdoorsy residents sail, cycle and run a few steps from the center of town.

Take this walk on Trips

Church Street Marketplace

Get a dose of urban culture at Church St Marketplace, the city's commercial and social hub. This attractive pedestrian zone is lined with shops, food carts, restaurants, cafes, street musicians, and climbing rocks that are popular with young children. It's packed with locals any time of day and is the epicenter of nightlife on weekends.

The Walk » Walk along the pedestrian mall. After College St, you will see your next stop on the right.

Firehouse Center for the Visual Arts

Burlington's community art center, **Firehouse Center for the Visual Arts** (www.burlingtoncityarts.com; 135 Church St; ⊘ noon-5pm Tue-Thu & Sun, noon-8pm Fri, 9am-8pm Sat), features Vermont artists, as well as those from further afield, with a focus on contemporary art.

The Walk » From Church St, turn right onto Main St. You'll immediately see the lake looming in front of you. Walk downhill; the road dead-ends at your next stop.

Union Station

The brick beaux arts–style structure (built in 1915) is **Union Station** (1 Main St), the former station for the Central Vermont railway; look for the quirky steel-winged monkeys looming on top of the building. Inside, admire the revolving local art; head downstairs to see murals detailing the history and development of Burlington, and a local artist's sculpture entitled *Train Ball*.

The Walk » Exit on the bottom floor and turn right. You'll pass the old platform, which looks like it could receive passengers anytime. Walk on the path following the tracks.

ECHO Lake Aquarium & Science Center

Nature-lovers, or those interested in green architecture, will definitely want to explore the **ECHO Lake Aquarium**

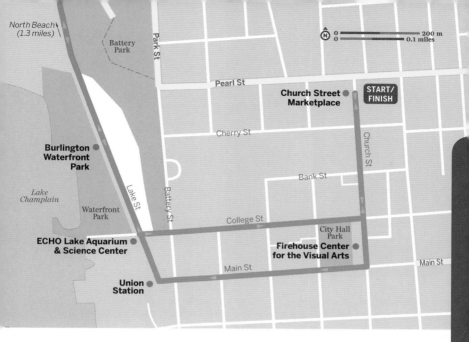

& Science Center (www.echovermont.org; 1 College St; adult/child 3-17yr $13.50/10.50; ⊙10am-5pm; 🐾), a waterfront science museum that is LEED-certified for its state-of-the-art environmentally friendly design. Focusing on Lake Champlain's ecosystem, it features a multitude of small aquariums and rotating science exhibits with plenty of hands-on, kid-friendly activities. Don't miss the Into the Lake exhibit which spotlights Champ, a local 'sea monster' allegedly dwelling in the lake.

The Walk)) Cross the roundabout and you'll see the boathouse off to the left and the boardwalk up ahead, both part of your next stop.

Burlington Waterfront Park

Refreshingly unencumbered by the souvenir stands that crowd the more developed waterfronts, this park has a low-key promenade with swinging four-person benches and swaths of grassy spots. Its marina contains **Splash at the Boathouse** (www.splashattheboathouse.com; College St; ⊙10am-2am mid-May–Sep), an outdoor restaurant and bar on a floating dock with stellar views over Lake Champlain. Perfect for kicking back with an evening cocktail, or a microbrew at sunset.

The Walk)) Walk down the boardwalk and continue past the sailing club to the Burlington Recreation Path, a paved path that takes you along the lake. The elevation increases slightly to give you excellent views from above.

North Beach

This wide stretch makes you feel like you've landed on a small ocean. Wriggle your feet in the sand, breathe in the crisp air and, if it's summer, dive in.

The Walk)) Return to the Burlington Recreation Path and walk back to the waterfront park. Then walk east along College St and north up Church St until you return to the Church St Marketplace.

Eat your way through food-and art-crazed Portland, one of America's coolest small cities; or venture into Maine's inland region, a vast wilderness of pine forest and mountain scenery.

Maine

Maine is New England's frontier – a land so vast it could swallow the region's five other states with scarcely a gulp. While time-honored fishing villages and seaside lobster joints are the fame of Maine, inland travel also offers ample reward. Maine's rugged interior is given over to rushing rivers, dense forests and lofty mountains just aching to be explored.

History

It's estimated that 20,000 Native Americans from tribes known collectively as Wabanaki (People of the Dawn) inhabited Maine when the first Europeans arrived. The French and English vied to establish colonies in Maine during the 1600s but, deterred by the harsh winters, these settlements failed.

In 1652 Massachusetts annexed the territory of Maine to provide a front line of defense against potential attacks during the French and Indian Wars. And indeed Maine at times did become a battlefield between English Colonists in New England and French forces in Canada. In the early 19th century, in an attempt to settle sparsely populated Maine, 100-acre homesteads were offered free to settlers willing to farm the land. In 1820 Maine broke from Massachusetts and entered the Union as a state.

In 1851 Maine became the first state to ban the sale of alcoholic beverages, the start of a temperance movement that eventually

took hold throughout the US. It wasn't until 1934 that Prohibition was finally lifted.

ⓘ Information

If you're entering the state on I-95 heading north, stop at the well-stocked visitor information center on the highway.

Maine Bureau of Parks and Land (☑800-332-1501; www.campwithme.com) Offers camping in 12 state parks.

Maine Office of Tourism (☑888-624-6345; www.visitmaine.com; 59 State House Station, Augusta) These folks maintain information centers on the principal routes into the state – Calais, Fryeburg, Hampden, Houlton, Kittery and Yarmouth. Each facility is open 9am to 5:30pm, with extended hours in summer. Many offer wi-fi.

Portland

The 18th-century poet Henry Wadsworth Longfellow referred to his childhood city as the 'jewel by the sea,' and, thanks to a hefty revitalization effort, Portland once again sparkles. Its lively waterfront, burgeoning gallery scene and manageable size add up to great exploring. Foodies, rev up your taste buds: cutting-edge cafes and chef-driven restaurants have turned Portland into the hottest dining scene north of Boston.

Portland sits on a hilly peninsula surrounded on three sides by water: Back Cove, Casco Bay and the Fore River. It's easy to find your way around. Commercial St (US 1A) runs along the waterfront through the Old Port, while the parallel Congress St is the main thoroughfare through downtown.

Sights

Old Port   NEIGHBORHOOD
Handsome 19th-century brick buildings line the streets of the Old Port, with Portland's most enticing shops, pubs and restaurants located within this five-square-block district. By night, flickering gas lanterns add to the atmosphere. What to do here? Eat some wicked fresh seafood, down a local microbrew, buy a nautical-themed T-shirt from an up-and-coming designer, or peruse the many tiny local art galleries. Don't forget to wander the authentically stinky wharfs, ducking into a fishmongers to order some lobsters.

Portland Museum of Art   MUSEUM
(☑207-775-6148; www.portlandmuseum.org; 7 Congress Sq; adult/child $12/6, 5-9pm Fri free; ☺10am-5pm Sat-Thu, to 9pm Fri, closed Mon mid-Oct–May) Founded in 1882, this well-respected museum houses an outstanding collection of American artists. Maine artists, including Winslow Homer, Edward Hopper, Louise Nevelson and Andrew Wyeth, are well represented. You'll also find a few works by European masters, including Degas, Picasso and Renoir. The majority of works are found in the postmodern Charles Shipman Payson building, designed by the firm of famed architect IM Pei.

Fort Williams Park   PARK
(☺sunrise-sunset) 🅿️ FREE Four miles southeast of Portland on Cape Elizabeth, 90-acre Fort Williams Park is worth visiting simply for the panoramas and picnic possibilities. Stroll around the ruins of the fort, a late-19th-century artillery base, checking out the WWII bunkers and gun emplacements (a German U-boat was spotted in Casco Bay in 1942) that still dot the rolling lawns. Strange as it may seem, the fort actively guarded the entrance to Casco Bay until 1964.

Adjacent to the fort stands the Portland Head Light, the oldest of Maine's 52 functioning lighthouses. It was commissioned by George Washington in 1791 and staffed until 1989, when machines took over. The keeper's house has been passed into service as the Museum at Portland Head Light (☑207-799-2661; www.portlandheadlight.com; 1000

Shore Rd; adult/child 6-18yr $2/1; ☺10am-4pm Jun-Oct), which traces the maritime and military history of the region.

Longfellow House   HISTORIC BUILDING
(☑207-879-0427; www.mainehistory.org; 489 Congress St; guided tour adult/child 7-17yr $15/3; ☺10am-5pm Mon-Sat, noon-5pm Sun May-Oct, closed Sun & Mon Nov-Apr) Visitors have been checking out dusty artifacts in the home of revered American poet Henry Wadsworth Longfellow for more than 110 years. It's a thought that can creep you out if you think about it too much while squinting at the framed needlepoint displays – just like the thousands who have squinted before you. Most now dead. But whatever.

Longfellow grew up in this Federal-style house, built in 1788 by his Revolutionary War hero grandfather. The house has been impeccably restored to look like it did in the 1800s, complete with original furniture and artifacts. Tours last one hour.

Activities

For a whole different angle on Portland and Casco Bay, hop one of the boats offering narrated scenic cruises out of Portland Harbor.

MAINE LEAF-PEEPS

Maine is better known for its coast than for its mountains, but inland Maine still offers its own array of superb colors. The best leaf-peeping route follows US 2 between Bethel (p118) and Rangeley Lake (see p119).

➡ The town of **Bethel** is a destination in and of itself and serves as a great base for hiking through the rainbow of colors in nearby Grafton Notch State Park.

➡ Primarily known as a winter ski resort, **Sunday River Ski Resort** (p47) also offers non-ski activities in the autumn such as chair-lift rides, ATV tours, canoeing and mountain biking. All boast fine views of the fall foliage.

➡ **Shelburne birches** (between Gilead and Shelburne on US 2) is also excellent for viewing the vibrant colors.

Casco Bay Lines CRUISE
(☑207-774-7871; www.cascobaylines.com; 56 Commercial St; adult $13-24, child $7-11) This outfit cruises the Casco Bay islands delivering mail, freight and visitors looking to bike or explore. It also offers cruises to Bailey Island (adult/child five to nine years old $26/12).

Maine Island Kayak Company KAYAKING
(☑207-766-2373; www.maineislandkayak.com; 70 Luther St, Peak Island; tour $65; ⊗May-Nov) On Peak Island, a 15-minute cruise from downtown on the Casco Bay Lines, this well-run outfitter offers fun day and overnight trips exploring the islands of Casco Bay.

Maine Brew Bus TOUR
(☑207-200-9111; www.themainebrewbus.com; tour $50-75; ⊗tour times vary) Hop aboard the green bus for tours and tastings at some of Portland's most beloved breweries and brewpubs, from Allagash to Sebago. Lunch at a brewpub is included on the Casco Fiasco tour.

Portland Schooner Company CRUISE
(☑207-766-2500; www.portlandschooner.com; 56 Commercial St; adult/child under 13yr $42/21; ⊗May-Oct) Offers tours aboard an elegant, early-20th-century schooner. In addition to two-hour sails, you can book overnight tours ($250 per person, including dinner and breakfast).

🛏 Sleeping

Portland has a healthy selection of midrange and upscale B&Bs, though very little at the budget end. The most idyllic accommodations are in the old town houses and grand Victorians in the West End.

Inn at St John INN $$
(☑207-773-6481; www.innatstjohn.com; 939 Congress St; r incl breakfast $125-275; P 🕏) On the western fringe of downtown, this turn-of-the-century hotel has a stuck-in-time feel, from the old-fashioned pigeonhole mailboxes behind the lobby desk to the narrow, sweetly floral rooms. Ask for a room away from noisy Congress St. The value rooms come with a private hall bath or shared hall bath. Book early for big weekends.

Morrill Mansion B&B $$
(☑207-774-6900; www.morrillmansion.com; 249 Vaughan St; r incl breakfast $169-239; 🕏) Charles Morrill, the original owner of this 19th-century West End town house, made his fortune by founding B&M baked beans, still a staple of Maine pantries. His home has been transformed into a handsome B&B, with eight guest rooms furnished in a trim, classic style. Think hardwood floors, and lots of tasteful khaki and taupe shades.

Some rooms are a bit cramped; if you need lots of space, try the two-room Morrill Suite.

Portland Harbor Hotel HOTEL $$$
(☑207-775-9090; www.portlandharborhotel.com; 468 Fore St; r from $339; P 🕏 🐾) This independent hotel has a classically coiffed lobby, where guests relax on upholstered leather chairs surrounding the glowing fireplace. The rooms carry on the classicism, with sunny gold walls and pert blue toile bedspreads. The windows face Casco Bay, the interior garden or the street; garden rooms are quieter. Parking is $18 (valet only). Pets are $25 per night.

🍴 Eating

Two Fat Cats Bakery BAKERY $
(☑207-347-5144; www.twofatcatsbakery.com; 47 India St; treats $3-7; ⊗8am-6pm Mon-Fri, to 5pm Sat, to 4pm Sun, closed Mon Jan & Feb) Tiny bakery serving pastries, pies, melt-in-your-

mouth chocolate-chip cookies and fabulous Whoopie Pies.

DuckFat
SANDWICHES $

([📱]207-774-8080; www.duckfat.com; 43 Middle St; small fries $5, sandwiches $10-14; ⊙11am-10pm) DuckFat has the best fries we've tasted in our many decades of fry-eating. No lie. Fried in – yes – duck fat, they're shatteringly crisp, with melt-in-your-mouth fluffy centers. Dipping sauces, like truffle ketchup, are good, but unnecessary. Panini are also excellent. But again, it's about the fries. Decor is 'hipster fast-food joint,' with a blackboard menu and a handful of bistro tables.

★ Green Elephant
VEGETARIAN $$

([📱]207-347-3111; www.greenelephantmaine.com; 608 Congress St; mains $10-15; ⊙11:30am-2:30pm & 5-9:30pm Mon-Sat, to 9pm Sun; [🍴]) They'll spice it as hot as you like it at this Zen-chic, Thai-inspired cafe, which serves brilliant vegetarian fare in an airy and spare nook downtown. Start with the crispy spinach wontons, then move on to one of the exotic soy creations like garlic and ginger tofu, or a flavorful curry such as the Panang coconut curry with vegetables.

Susan's Fish & Chips
SEAFOOD $$

([📱]207-878-3240; www.susansfishnchips.com; 1135 Forest Ave/US 302; mains $9-22; ⊙11am-8pm) Pop in for chowder and fish and chips at this no-fuss, welcoming eatery on US 302, where the tartar sauce comes in mason jars. Located in a former garage.

J's Oyster
SEAFOOD $$

([📱]207-772-4828; www.jsoyster.com; 5 Portland Pier; sandwiches $5-18, mains $25-31; ⊙11:30am-11pm) Maybe not the friendliest place on the planet, but this well-loved dive has the cheapest raw oysters in town. Eat 'em on the deck overlooking the pier. The oyster-averse have plenty of sandwiches and seafood mains to choose from.

★ Fore Street
NEW AMERICAN $$$

([📱]207-775-2717; www.forestreet.biz; 288 Fore St; small plates $13-22, mains $28-40; ⊙5:30-10pm Sun-Thu, to 10:30pm Fri & Sat) Roasting is a high art at Fore Street, one of Maine's most lauded restaurants. Chickens turn on spits in the open kitchen as chefs slide iron kettles of mussels into the wood-burning oven. Local, seasonal eating is taken very seriously, and the menu changes daily to offer what's freshest. The large, noisy dining room nods to its warehouse past with exposed brick and pine paneling.

Offerings may include a fresh pea salad, periwinkles (a local shellfish) in herbed cream, or roast bluefish with pancetta. The chilled and smoked seafood platter, offered daily, is a palate pleaser. Reservations needed, but you may be able to snag a bar seat between 5:30pm and 6pm.

MAINE

Old Port (p115)

Drinking & Entertainment

Gritty McDuff's Brew Pub BREWPUB
(www.grittys.com; 396 Fore St; ⊙11am-1am) Gritty is an apt description for this party-happy Old Port pub. You'll find a generally raucous crowd drinking excellent beers – Gritty brews its own award-winning ales downstairs.

Port City Music Hall CONCERT HALL
(☑207-956-6000; www.portcitymusichall.com; 504 Congress St) This three-story performance space hosts big-name and smaller-name bands.

Shopping

For boutiques, galleries and craft shops, head downtown to Exchange and Fore Sts in Old Port.

Portland Farmers Market FARMERS MARKET
(http://portlandmainefarmersmarket.org; ⊙7am-noon Sat, to 1pm Mon & Wed May-Nov) Vendors hawk everything from Maine blueberries to homemade pickles on Saturdays in summer and fall in Deering Oaks Park downtown (Park Ave at Forest Ave). On Monday and Wednesday the market is in Monument Sq on Congress St. Saturdays only in winter at 200 Anderson St.

Harbor Fish Market FISHMONGER
(☑207-775-0251; www.harborfish.com; 9 Custom House Wharf; ⊙8:30am-5:30pm Mon-Sat, 9am-noon Sun) On Custom House Wharf, this iconic fishmonger packs lobsters and seafood for road trips, island trips, and flights; it ships to anywhere in the US.

Maine Potters Market POTTERY
(www.mainepottersmarket.com; 376 Fore St; ⊙10am-9pm daily) A cooperatively owned gallery featuring the work of a dozen or so different Maine ceramists.

ⓘ Information

Greater Portland Convention & Visitors Bureau (www.visitportland.com; Ocean Gateway Bldg, 14 Ocean Gateway Pier; ⊙9am-5pm Mon-Fri, to 4pm Sat & Sun Jun-Oct, hours vary rest of year) Stop by for brochures and maps.

ⓘ Getting There & Around

Portland International Jetport (PWM; ☑207-874-8877; www.portlandjetport.org) has non-stop flights to cities in the eastern US.

Greyhound (www.greyhound.com; 950 Congress St) buses and **Amtrak** (☑800-872-7245; www.amtrak.com; 100 Thompson's Point Rd)

trains connect Portland and Boston; both take about 2½ hours and charge $14 to $34 one way.

The local bus **Metro** (www.gpmetrobus.com; fares $1.50), which runs throughout the city, has its main terminus at Monument Sq, the intersection of Elm and Congress Sts.

Interior Maine

Sparsely populated northern and western Maine is rugged outdoor country. River rafting, hiking trails up Maine's highest mountain and the ski town of Bethel make the region a magnet for adventurers.

Bethel

The rural community of Bethel, nestled in the rolling Maine woods 12 miles east of New Hampshire on ME 26, offers an engaging combination of mountain scenery, outdoor escapades and good-value accommodations. **Bethel Area Chamber of Commerce** (☑207-824-2282; www.bethelmaine.com; 8 Station Pl; ⊙9am-5pm Jun–mid-Oct, closed Sat & Sun mid-Oct-May) provides information for visitors.

Activities

Bethel Outdoor Adventure KAYAKING
(☑207-824-4224; www.betheloutdooradventure.com; 121 Mayville Rd/US 2; per day kayak/canoe $46/67; ⊙8am-6pm mid-May–mid-Oct) This downtown outfitter rents canoes, kayaks and bicycles. It also arranges lessons, guided trips, and shuttles to and from the Androscoggin River.

Grafton Notch State Park HIKING
See p47.

Sunday River Ski Resort HIKING, SKIING
See p47.

🛏 Sleeping

Chapman Inn B&B $
(☑207-824-2657; www.chapmaninn.com; 2 Church St; dm/ste incl breakfast $35/139 r incl breakfast $89-129; ❋ 🛜) This roomy downtown guesthouse has character in spades. The nine private rooms are done up in florals and antiques, with slightly sloping floors attesting to the home's age. In winter skiers bunk down in the snug dorm, complete with a wood-paneled game room presided over by a massive mounted moose head. Breakfast is a lavish spread of homemade pastries and made-to-order omelets.

Sudbury Inn & Suds Pub
INN **$$**

(☑ 207-824-2174; www.sudburyinn.com; 151 Main St; r incl breakfast $119-139, ste incl breakfast $189-199; ☺ pub from 11:30am daily, restaurant 5:30-9pm Thu-Sat; ☒) The choice place to stay in downtown Bethel, this historic inn has 17 rooms, a pub with 29 beers on tap, pizza and live weekend entertainment. It also has an excellent dinner restaurant serving Maine-centric fare (mains $20 to $34).

Eating

Cho Sun
ASIAN **$$**

(☑ 207-824-7370; www.chosunrestaurant.com; 141 Main St; mains $17-27, sushi from $7; ☺ 5-9pm Wed-Sun) Korea smashes into Maine at this unassuming Victorian house. Try dishes from the owner's native South Korea, such as bibimbap (rice pot with meat and vegetables) or kimchi stew. There's also a sushi bar.

Café DiCocoa
CAFE **$**

(www.cafedicocoa.com; 119 Main St; mains under $8; ☺ 7am-6pm daily Jul-early Oct, Thu-Sun low season, closed Nov, Apr & May; ☑) This funky orange bungalow is a morning must for espresso-based drinks. It also serves wholegrain baked goods and vegetarian lunches.

Good Food Store
SANDWICHES, SELF-CATERING **$**

(www.goodfoodbethel.com; 212 Mayville Rd/ME 26; salads & sandwiches under $7, heat & eat meals $10-15; ☺ store 9am-8pm, takeout 11am-6pm) Buy sandwiches, salads and heat-and-eat meals at this gourmet organic market and wine shop. The homemade cookies and dried fruit are fantastic. BBQ by Smokin' Good BBQ is sold here Thursday through Sunday.

❶ Getting There & Away

Bethel lies 70 miles north of Portland, via ME 26 . If you're heading into the White Mountains of New Hampshire, take US 2 east from Bethel toward Gorham (22 miles) and head south to North Conway.

Rangeley Lake & Around

Surrounded by mountains and thick hardwood forests, the Rangeley Lake region is a marvelous year-round destination for adventurers. The gateway to the alpine scenery is the laid-back town of Rangeley.

During the early 20th century the lakes in this region were dotted with vast frame hotels and peopled with vacationers from Boston, New York and Philadelphia. Though most of the great hotels are gone, the reasons for coming here remain.

Activities

The mountains around Rangeley offer good skiing and snowboarding options.

Sugarloaf
SKIING

See p50.

▦ Sleeping & Eating

Rangeley Inn
INN **$$**

(☑ 207-864-3341; www.therangeleyinn.com; 2443 Main St; r $115-175) Relax by the fire and admire the mounted bear in the lobby of this big creaky turn-of-the-century lodge. Rooms are simple and old-fashioned, with Victorian floral wallpaper and brass beds.

Loon Lodge
LODGE **$$**

(☑ 207-864-5666; www.loonlodgeme.com; 16 Pickford Rd; r incl breakfast $110-165; ☎) Hidden in the woods by the lake, this log-cabin lodge has nine rooms, most with a backwoods-chic look, with wood-plank walls and handmade quilts.

Red Onion
ITALIAN **$$**

(www.rangeleyredonion.com; 2511 Main St; mains $12-17; ☺ 11am-9pm; ☒) A big plate of chicken parmesan after a day on the slopes has been a Rangeley tradition for four decades. This boisterous Italian-American joint is also known for its pizzas and its 1970s wood-paneled bar.

❶ Information

The **Rangeley Lakes Chamber of Commerce** (☑ 207-864-5364; www.rangeleymaine.com; 6 Park Rd; ☺ 9am-5pm Mon-Sat), just off Main St, can answer questions.

❶ Getting There & Away

Rangeley is about 2½ hours north of Portland by car, on the northeast side of Rangeley Lake. From I-95, take ME 4 N to ME 108 W, then take ME 17 W to 4 S.

Sabbathday Lake

The nation's only active Shaker community is at Sabbathday Lake, 25 miles north of Portland. Founded in the early 18th century, a handful of devotees keep the Shaker tradition of simple living, hard work and fine artistry alive. You can tour several of their buildings on a visit to the **Shaker Museum** (☑ 207-926-4597; www.maineshakers.com; adult/child 6-12yr $10/2; ☺ 10am-4:30pm Mon-Sat late May–mid-Oct). To get there, take exit 63 off the Maine Turnpike and continue north for 8 miles on ME 26.

Driving in New England

Let us answer all your questions about driving in New England, including where to pahk your cah.

Driving Fast Facts

➡ **Right or left?** Drive on the right
➡ **Legal driving age** 16
➡ **Top speed limit** 75mph (on interstate in rural Maine)
➡ **Best bumper sticker** 'Wicked Cool Bumpah Stickah'

DRIVER'S LICENSE & DOCUMENTS

All drivers must carry a driver's license, the car registration and proof of insurance. If your license is not in English, you will need an official translation or an International Driving Permit (IDP). You will also need a credit card in order to rent a car.

INSURANCE

Liability All drivers are required to obtain a minimum amount of liability insurance, which would cover the damage that you might cause to other people and property in case of an accident. Liability insurance can be purchased from rental-car companies for about $12 per day.

Collision For damage to the rental vehicle, a collision damage waiver (CDW) is available from the rental company for about $18 a day.

Alternative sources Your personal auto insurance may extend to rental cars, so it's worth investigating before purchasing liability or collision from the rental company. Additionally, some credit cards offer reimbursement coverage for collision damages if you rent the car with that credit card; again, check before departing. Most credit-card coverage isn't valid for rentals of more than 15 days or for exotic models, SUVs, vans and 4WD vehicles.

RENTING A CAR

Rental cars are readily available at regional airports and in major towns. Rates usually include unlimited mileage. Dropping off the car at a different location from where you picked it up usually incurs an additional fee. It always pays to shop around between rental companies, utilizing price-comparison websites.

Renting a car without a major credit card is difficult, if not impossible. Without one, some agencies simply will not rent vehicles, while others require prepayment, a deposit slightly higher than the cost of your rental, pay stubs, proof of round-trip airfare and more.

The following companies operate in New England:

Alamo (www.goalamo.com)
Avis (www.avis.com)
Budget (www.budget.com)
Dollar (www.dollarcar.com)

Enterprise (www.enterprise.com)

Hertz (www.hertz.com)

National (www.nationalcar.com)

Rent-A-Wreck (www.rentawreck.com)
Rents cars that may have more wear and tear than your typical rental vehicle, but are actually far from wrecks.

Thrifty (www.thrifty.com)

BORDER CROSSING

Generally, crossing the US–Canada border is straightforward. The biggest hassle is usually the length of the lines. All travelers entering the USA are required to carry passports, including citizens of Canada and the USA.

MAPS

Detailed state-highway maps are distributed free by state governments. You can call or write to state tourism offices in advance to request maps, or you can pick up the maps at highway tourism information offices (welcome centers) when you enter a state on a major highway.

Road-Trip Websites

American Automobile Association (AAA; www.aaa.com) Provides maps and other information, as well as travel discounts and emergency assistance for members.

Gas Buddy (www.gasbuddy.com) Find the cheapest gas in town.

New England Travel Planner (www.newenglandtravelplanner. com) Routes, reviews and other travel resources.

Traffic.com (www.traffic.com) Real-time traffic reports, with details about accidents and traffic jams.

Another excellent map resource is **DeLorme Mapping Company** (www. delorme.com), which publishes individual state maps – atlas-style books with detailed coverage of backcountry roads. The scales range from 1:65,000 to 1:135,000. The New England box set includes all six states for $62.

Road Distances (miles)

	Boston, MA	Provincetown, MA	Portsmouth, NH	Portland, ME	Bar Harbor, ME	Burlington, VT	Brattleboro, VT	Norwich, VT/ Hanover, NH	Hartford, CT
Provincetown, MA	114								
Portsmouth, NH	58	171							
Portland, ME	108	221	51						
Bar Harbor, ME	267	380	210	159					
Burlington, VT	217	330	207	209	334				
Brattleboro, VT	120	220	124	175	354	151			
Norwich, VT/Hanover, NH	127	240	116	167	346	96	69		
Hartford, CT	101	206	150	201	380	236	85	152	
Providence, RI	50	120	106	157	336	265	137	175	86

ROADS & CONDITIONS

New England roads are very good – even the warren of hard-packed dirt roads that crisscross Vermont. A few hazards to be aware of:

➡ Some of the region's big, old cities can be difficult to navigate. Boston in particular is notorious for its scofflaw drivers and maddening maze of one-way streets. Park your car and use public transport to get around.

➡ Traffic is heavy around urban areas during rush hour (7am to 9am and 4pm to 7pm Monday through Friday).

➡ Some roads across northern mountain passes in Vermont, New Hampshire and Maine are closed during the winter, but good signage gives you plenty of warning.

Toll Roads

You are likely to encounter tolls for some roads, bridges and tunnels while driving around New England:

➡ Blue Star Turnpike (New Hampshire Turnpike; I-95)

➡ Claiborne Pell Newport Bridge, Rhode Island

➡ Frederick E Everett Turnpike (Central New Hampshire Turnpike)

➡ Maine Turnpike (I-95)

➡ Massachusetts Turnpike (I-90)

➡ Mt Equinox Skyline Dr, Vermont

➡ Mt Mansfield Auto Toll Rd, Vermont

➡ Mt Washington Auto Rd, New Hampshire

➡ Spaulding Turnpike, New Hampshire

➡ Sumner Tunnel, Massachusetts

➡ Ted Williams Tunnel, Massachusetts

➡ Tobin Bridge (Mystic River Bridge), Massachusetts

New England Playlist

Sweet Baby James James Taylor

The Impression that I Get The Mighty Mighty Bosstones

Farmhouse Phish

New Hampshire Matt Pond PA

Let the Good Times Roll The Cars

ROAD RULES

The maximum speed limit on most New England interstates is 65mph, but some have a limit of 55mph. (One stretch of I-95 in rural Maine has a speed limit of 75mph.) On undivided highways, the speed limit will vary from 30mph to 55mph. Police enforce speed limits by patrolling in police cruisers and in unmarked cars. Fines can cost upwards of $350 in Connecticut, and it's similarly expensive in other states.

Other road rules:

➡ Driving laws are different in each of the New England states, but most require the use of seat belts.

➡ In every state, children under four years of age must be placed in a child safety seat secured by a seat belt.

➡ Most states require motorcycle riders to wear helmets whenever they ride. In any case, use of a helmet is highly recommended.

➡ All six New England states prohibit texting while driving, while Connecticut has banned all handheld cell-phone use by drivers.

PARKING

Public parking is readily available in most New England destinations, whether on the street or in parking lots. In rural areas and small towns, it is often free of charge. Many towns have metered parking, which will limit the amount of time you can leave your car (usually two hours or more).

Parking can be a challenge in urban areas, especially Boston. Street parking is limited, so you will probably have to pay for parking in private lots.

FUEL

Gas stations are ubiquitous and many are open 24 hours a day. Small-town stations may be open only from 7am to 8pm or 9pm.

Most stations require that you pay before you pump. More modern pumps have credit-/debit-card terminals built into them, so you can pay with plastic right at the pump. At 'full-service' stations, an attendant will pump your gas for you; no tip is expected.

Driving Problem-Buster

What should I do if my car breaks down? Call the service number provided by the rental-car company, and it will make arrangements with a local garage. If you're driving your own car, it's advisable to join the AAA (see p121), which provides emergency assistance.

What if I have an accident? If any damage is incurred, you'll have to call the local police (☑911) to come to the scene of the accident and file an accident report, for insurance purposes.

What should I do if I get stopped by the police? Always pull over to the right at the first available opportunity. Stay in your car and roll down the window. Show the police officer your driver's license and automobile registration. For any violations, you cannot pay the officer issuing the ticket; rather, payment must be made by mail or by internet.

How do the tolls work? Most tolls are payable in cash only. Tolling stations are usually staffed, so exact change is not required. Alternatively, consider purchasing an E-Z Pass for the state you will be traveling in (this is not transferable to other states).

What if I can't find anywhere to stay? In summer and autumn, it's advisable to make reservations in advance. Most towns have tourist information centers or chambers of commerce that will help travelers find accommodation in a pinch.

SAFETY

New England does not present any particular safety concerns for drivers. That said, travelers are advised to always remove valuables and lock all car doors, especially in urban areas.

Be extra cautious driving at night on rural roads, which may not be well lit and may be populated by deer, moose and other creatures that can total your car if you hit them the wrong way.

RADIO

Maine WCYY (94.3FM) plays oldies and newbies out of Portland, with Alternative Mornings from 6am till noon.

Massachusetts Boston is blessed with two public radio stations – WGBH (89.7FM) and WBUR (90.9FM) – broadcasting news, classical music and radio shows.

New Hampshire The Freewaves (91.3FM) is run by the students of the University of New Hampshire, offering indie, classical, jazz and folk.

Vermont WRUV (90.1 FM) – also known as Burlington's Better Alternative – is a nonprofit student- and volunteer-run radio station, playing a mix of music at DJs' discretion, but no songs that were EVER in Billboard's Hot 100 can be played.

FERRY CROSSINGS

Unfortunately, you can't drive to New England's offshore islands. Park your car in port ($10 to $20 per day) and hop on a boat. In addition to the high-speed catamarans listed below, Hy-Line and Steamship also offer traditional ferry crossings (half the price but twice the time). They can also bring your car ($400 to $450), but you'll need to book well in advance.

Block Island Ferry (www.blockislandferry. com) Ferry between Point Judith, RI, and Block Island, RI. Car-and-passenger ferries take an hour; high-speed passenger ferries ($36 round-trip) take 30 minutes.

Downeast Windjammer (www.downeast windjammer.com; adult/child $30/20, bikes $6) Passenger-only ferry between Bar Harbor, ME, and Winter Harbor, ME, allowing exploration of the island and mainland sections of Acadia National Park.

Steamship Authority (www.steamship authority.com; South St; round-trip adult/child $67/34) Catamaran between Hyannis, MA, and Nantucket, MA.

BEHIND THE SCENES

SEND US YOUR FEEDBACK

We love to hear from travelers – your comments help make our books better. We read every word, and we guarantee that your feedback goes straight to the authors. Visit **lonelyplanet. com/contact** to submit your updates and suggestions.

Note: We may edit, reproduce and incorporate your comments in Lonely Planet products such as guidebooks, websites and digital products, so let us know if you don't want your comments reproduced or your name acknowledged. For a copy of our privacy policy visit lonelyplanet.com/privacy.

ACKNOWLEDGMENTS

Climate map data adapted from Peel MC, Finlayson BL & McMahon TA (2007) 'Updated World Map of the Köppen-Geiger Climate Classification', *Hydrology and Earth System Sciences*, 11, 163344.

Cover photographs: Front: Autumn countryside in the Green Mountains, Ron Thomas/Getty; Back: Lake Champlain barn, Vermont, George Robinson/ Alamy

THIS BOOK

This 1st edition of *New England Fall Foliage Road Trips* was researched and written by Amy C Balfour, Gregor Clark, Ned Friary, Paula Hardy, Caroline Sieg and Mara Vorhees. This guidebook was produced by the following:

Destination Editor Rebecca Warren

Product Editor Kate Chapman

Senior Cartographer Alison Lyall

Book Designer Wibowo Rusli

Cartographers Mick Garrett, Julie Sheridan, Diana von Holdt

Assisting Editors Imogen Bannister, Catherine Naghten

Cover Researcher Naomi Parker

Thanks to Shahara Ahmed, Anita Banh, Brendan Dempsey, James Hardy, Katherine Marsh, Darren O'Connell, Katie O'Connell, Kirsten Rawlings, Angela Tinson

OUR STORY

A beat-up old car, a few dollars in the pocket and a sense of adventure. In 1972 that's all Tony and Maureen Wheeler needed for the trip of a lifetime – across Europe and Asia overland to Australia. It took several months, and at the end – broke but inspired – they sat at their kitchen table writing and stapling together their first travel guide, *Across Asia on the Cheap*. Within a week they'd sold 1500 copies. Lonely Planet was born.

Today, Lonely Planet has offices in Melbourne, London and Oakland, with more than 600 staff and writers. We share Tony's belief that 'a great guidebook should do three things: inform, educate and amuse'.

INDEX

INDEX D–M

000 Map pages

OUR WRITERS

PAULA HARDY

The British half of an American-British couple, Paula spends a lot of time hopping across the pond, torn between the bright lights of London town and Boston, where weekending in the New England countryside is a near-weekly activity. Research has taken her way off the beaten path into Connecticut's dairy barns, lobster shacks (yum!) and wine-tasting rooms, and Rhode Island's tiny East Bay villages and breezy Block Island cycling trails – the lasting memories of Baggo defeats and Mudslide sundowners won't be easily forgotten.

AMY C BALFOUR

Amy has hiked, biked and paddled her way across the US. Raised in the South, she's been visiting the Outer Banks since childhood and has backpacked along the Appalachian Trail in the Great Smokies. In New Hampshire she explored the White Mountains and tackled Mt Monadnock for the first time. She has authored 26 guidebooks for Lonely Planet and has written for *Backpacker*, *Redbook*, *Southern Living* and the *Washington Post*.

CAROLINE SIEG

Caroline's relationship with New England began when she briefly lived in Boston. Subsequent trips to the region yielded countless hikes in the Green Mountains, excessive beer and cheese tasting in Vermont, and a profound obsession with blueberry pie and apple-cider doughnuts. She also believes that one of the best ways to embrace the area is to explore its ubiquitous lakes and waterways by boat. These days, she visits New England as often as she can.

GREGOR CLARK

Gregor fell in love with Vermont at age 16, while working as a summer conservation volunteer in the state's southwestern corner. His long-held dreams of moving to the Green Mountain State came to fruition in 1997, and he's been here ever since. A lifelong polyglot with a degree in Romance languages, Gregor has written regularly for Lonely Planet since 2000, with a focus on Europe and Latin America. He lives with his wife and two daughters in Middlebury, Vermont.

MARA VORHEES

Born and raised in St Clair Shores, Michigan, Mara traveled the world (if not the universe) before finally settling in the Hub. She spent several years pushing papers and tapping keys at Harvard University, but she has since embraced the life of a full-time travel writer, covering destinations as diverse as Russia and Belize. She lives in a pink house in Somerville, Massachusetts, with her husband, two kiddies and two kitties. She is often seen eating doughnuts in Union Sq and pedaling her bike along the Charles River. The pen-wielding traveler is the author of Lonely Planet's *Boston* guide, among other titles. Follow her adventures online at www.havetwinswilltravel.com.

NED FRIARY

Ned's college days were spent in Amherst, and traveling around his old stomping grounds always feels like a homecoming of sorts. He now lives on Cape Cod and has explored the region from one end to the other, searching out the best lobster roll, canoeing the marshes, and hiking and cycling the trails.

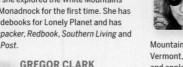

Published by Lonely Planet Publications Pty Ltd
ABN 36 005 607 983
1st edition – May 2016
ISBN 978 1 76034 0483
© Lonely Planet 2016   Photographs © as indicated 2016
10 9 8 7 6 5 4 3 2 1
Printed in China

Although the authors and Lonely Planet have taken all reasonable care in preparing this book, we make no warranty about the accuracy or completeness of its content and, to the maximum extent permitted, disclaim all liability arising from its use.